LOOK BOTH WAYS

**Helping Your Children
Stay Innocent
& Grow Wise**

Dan & Elizabeth Hamilton

InterVarsity Press
Downers Grove, Illinois

InterVarsity Press

P.O. Box 1400, Downers Grove, IL 60515
World Wide Web: www.ivpress.com
E-mail: mail@ivpress.com

©1999 by Dan and Elizabeth Hamilton

InterVarsity Press® is the book-publishing division of InterVarsity Christian Fellowship/USA®, a student movement active on campus at hundreds of universities, colleges and schools of nursing in the United States of America, and a member movement of the International Fellowship of Evangelical Students. For information about local and regional activities, write Public Relations Dept., InterVarsity Christian Fellowship/USA, 6400 Schroeder Rd., P.O. Box 7895, Madison, WI 53707-7895.

Cover photograph: Ariel Skelley/The Stock Market

ISBN 0-8308-1921-5

Printed in the United States of America ♾

Library of Congress Cataloging-in-Publication Data

Hamilton, Dan.
    Look both ways: helping your children stay innocent while growing
wise/ Dan and Elizabeth Hamilton.
        p.   cm.
    Includes bibliographical references.
    ISBN 0-8308-1921-5 (alk. paper)
        1. Parenting—Religious aspects—Christianity.   2. Christian
education—Home training.   3. Children—Religious life.
I. Hamilton, Elizabeth Guignard.   II. Title
BV4529.H297   1999
248.8'45—dc21   99-15060
                                                                              CIP

20	19	18	17	16	15	14	13	12	11	10	9	8	7	6	5	4	3	2	1
15	14	13	12	11	10	09	08	07	06	05	04	03	02	01	00	99			

for our parents
Jonathan Guignard
Marjorie Guignard
Chester C. Hamilton
Fern Hamilton

and their ancestors

and our loyal friends
who have given us
timely support and wise counsel

* * * *

I will open my mouth in parables,
I will utter hidden things, things from of old—
what we have heard and known,
what our fathers have told us. . . .

We will tell the next generation
the praiseworthy deeds of the LORD,
his power, and the wonders he has done.
PSALM 78:2-4

Introduction

The title for this book is not *How to Raise Great Kids*. We won't know for at least another ten years how our children finally turn out. (As we're writing this, our children are nine and twelve.) This book *is* about the principles and methods we are using to prepare them for independent life in a world that has been darkened and distorted by sin and made dangerous in a number of subtle and frightening ways.

Nor does this book address problems concerning troubled teens. We don't have teenagers yet, and the clouds foreshadowing hormone storms and the painful transition to adulthood are just beginning to appear on the horizon. This book is foundational and doesn't provide quick fixes for emergency applications. It is prevention rather than cure, and we have provided some of our philosophy as a background for the stories and insights.

Looking back at this compilation, the steps we've taken seem simple—not easy, mind you, but simple. These actions weren't (and couldn't have been) instituted all at once, for we learned them along with our children. There is a rational structure behind and beneath it all; applying the specific techniques we mention without implementing the underlying philosophy may lead to some disappointments. However, we feel that what we have done with and for our young children can only help ease certain difficulties and troubles in the years to come.

What makes us think we could write this book?

1. We have two children. They've lived with us every day of their lives and have subjected our theories to the relentless reality of their existence. ("How did you do your research for this book?" a friend asked Dan. "We had kids," he answered.)

2. Our children seem to us to be more than okay. We like who they are and what they do, and enjoy them as friends and companions rather than small household mammals which must be fed and (hopefully) trained. (Of course they're not perfect—they have to be separated from each other at odd intervals, reminded and redirected frequently, and occasionally hollered at.)

3. Our children seem to others to be more than okay. Neighbors enjoy their visits and borrow them for babysitting, dog walking, gardening work, snow removal, flyer delivery and other simple services. Other adults comment on their exemplary behavior and poise. They have been welcomed into stores where children generally are regarded with suspicion and misgivings.

4. We talk with others, listen, observe and read. We've seen the ways other parents have raised their children, and we've seen the results, both good and bad. We trust them, and our trust seems to be shared by other adults.

But we can't claim the credit for our "success," for equally valid reasons.

1. We started with good material. Both pregnancies were reasonably normal, the children were in fine health, and childhood progressed with no exceptional medical problems beyond Jennifer's milk allergies and recurrent asthma.

2. We had good (though certainly not perfect) family conditions ourselves. We both were Christians who had been raised in Christian homes. Dan had a full-time job, and our debts were few. Elizabeth

worked a few jobs out of the home and did custom sewing, but out of choice rather than necessity. We hadn't married young (Elizabeth was twenty-four, Dan twenty-seven) and didn't become parents right away (Elizabeth was twenty-nine and Dan thirty-two at Jennifer's birth). We had time to establish a stable home before adding to the family.

Yet on the negative side, we had a very limited network of family support. Dan's parents were twenty-five miles away but had some health restrictions. Elizabeth's family lived nine hundred miles away, across the Canadian border, and her father was fighting a losing battle against cancer. There was no regular involvement with our siblings, who were at least a hundred miles away. At the same time Dan was struggling with chronic depression, and we had endured the disintegration of three different churches.

3. We inherited multiple blessings. We are privileged to be the descendants of many Christians and are the beneficiaries of the lifestyles they maintained. Our family has not directly suffered the effects of alcoholism and other substance abuse, gambling, marital unfaithfulness or laziness. Just as the sins of the parents visit the following generations (Deuteronomy 5:9), so does the obedience of the parents. Our children are blessed because we love God and honor him. As our grandchildren will be blessed through our children, so our children have been blessed by their ancestors. Proverbs 17:6 puts it this way: "Children's children are a crown to the aged, and parents are the pride of their children."

And we have to confess that we weren't sure we were ready to have children. Would we like it? Would we be good at it? Would we raise happy, healthy, productive, godly children? Several years passed before we accepted the challenge, partly because we felt that we would be better people for the process. If we never cared for a child, sat up at night with a sick one, laughed and cried with our own offspring, prayed for them and wondered about them, we would be missing a tremendous opportunity for God to grow us up. We weren't sure we would like ourselves in thirty years, left to our own ways.

So here we are—content, though not completely satisfied. We have not become experts on children in general, or yours in particular. We are, however, becoming experts on *our* kids!

Originally these lessons were developed by Dan for a joint youth-adult Sunday-school class at Tabernacle Presbyterian Church in Indianapolis. As several parents asked for copies of the material we put together, the assembled notes began to look more and more like a book . . . and our friends at InterVarsity Press agreed. Enjoy; may these words help equip or reinvigorate you for the parenting adventure.

Warning: The stories you are about to read are true. In some places the names or details have been changed to protect the guilty and the easily embarrassed.

—1—

The Hardest
Part of
Parenting

*The heartbreaking beauty of childlike innocence
drives us to protect our children while still
allowing them to grow up. But in order
to protect them, we have to teach them about evil
and prepare them to face it on their own.
Fortunately, the Bible gives us commands
concerning wisdom, innocence, understanding
and our place as God's people in a world that
is turned away from him.*

Jennifer was sleeping, and I (Dan) stood beside her bed and *marveled over her. My firstborn, just two and a half years old. Her dark hair fanned out over the pillow and framed her glowing face—a Norman Rockwell print come to life.*

Then I looked past her, out the window at the world beyond. And my heart began to break, for I suddenly began to realize how it would be my job to prepare this unspoiled child for that waiting and wanton world.

She had never met a stranger; she greeted any passerby with a beaming smile and her life story. I would have to teach her, somehow, that there were people and powers she couldn't and mustn't trust— people who could deliberately hurt her, abuse her, destroy her goodness and even take her life.

She was ready to enjoy the world and absorb everything in it, looking for an endless and unquestioned supply of wholly good things. I would have to teach her, somehow, that there were other kinds of poisons than the bottles locked up over the dryer, other kinds of mortal danger that bore no warning labels, a dark supply of seeming joys that could only lead to sorrow.

Nor would that be the end of the matter. My wife Elizabeth, asleep in the next room, was approaching her time to bring our second child into the world—our son, as it would happen, Andrew. The task would begin anew, with a second tiny person to be loved, instructed, cuddled, corrected, shaped and eventually turned loose in the world.

The task, of course, was not only Dan's, though it seemed that way on that night of recognition and reckoning; it was Elizabeth's as well, and our parents', and that of anyone who took care of the children.

Elizabeth echoed these sentiments and fears and hopes in a diary she kept for each child against the day they would be old enough to understand and appreciate them.

(Sixteen weeks before Andrew's birth) *It's a crazy and violent world out here, little one. Sometimes it frightens me because I feel so vulnerable. When I remember that God really IS in control, then it's easier to confess the fact that this society and this world are slowly self-destructing. Some people don't want to have any children because all they see is futility and very little future. Yes, I see that too, but I know that my Father in heaven is so much bigger and stronger than violence, pollution, abortion, crime, laziness, politics and "natural disasters," and that my responsibility as his daughter is to continue along in life and not shrink from the responsibilities he gives me. And you are one of those responsibilities. I will do my best to be a good and godly mother to you and will raise you to know and love God and to delight in following and serving him.*

(Andrew's infant dedication, at three months of age) *Andrew, I pray for you: that you will be kept safe—physically and emotionally, that you will be healthy and strong, that you will be a man of impeccable standards, and above all that you will be a man of God,*

*following him, seeking him, searching after the truth of life that is
all around us.*

Doves and Serpents

Watching our children playing and sleeping, we were both charmed
and frightened by their innocence. Charmed because they were
lovely creatures God had temporarily placed in our custody. He was
actually trusting us with the job of raising them! Frightened
because we knew their uninformed innocence could not last
against the onslaught of the world, and it was largely our responsibility to equip them for the encounter. We kept returning to
Matthew 10:16 when we thought about our innocents and their
innocence: "Behold, I send you out as sheep in the midst of wolves;
so be wise as serpents and innocent as doves" (RSV).

No sermon heard or article read had satisfied us about the
meaning and application of this passage. The words are straight
from the lips of Jesus—but why would he have cause to commend
any part of the character of the serpent? Why would he bid his
people be like these legless worms that crawl about in the dust?
And anyway, how *can* we be like *both* doves *and* serpents at the
same time?

Whatever the answer, it is presented as a *command* and not a
choice. Therefore, we must understand it, or miss part of our calling
and our discipleship.

Another passage, puzzling in itself, helped explain this one. In
the surprising episode of Luke 16:1-9 Jesus describes the cleverness and understanding of a man faced with a dilemma:

> Jesus told his disciples: "There was a rich man whose manager was
> accused of wasting his possessions. So he called him in and asked
> him, 'What is this I hear about you? Give an account of your
> management, because you cannot be manager any longer.'
>
> "The manager said to himself, 'What shall I do now? My master
> is taking away my job. I'm not strong enough to dig, and I'm ashamed
> to beg—I know what I'll do so that, when I lose my job here, people

will welcome me into their houses.'

"So he called in each one of his master's debtors. He asked the first, 'How much do you owe my master?'

" 'Eight hundred gallons of olive oil,' he replied.

"The manager told him, 'Take your bill, sit down quickly, and make it four hundred.'

"Then he asked the second, 'And how much do you owe?'

" 'A thousand bushels of wheat,' he replied.

"He told him, 'Take your bill and make it eight hundred.'

"The master commended the dishonest manager because he had acted shrewdly. For the people of this world are more shrewd in dealing with their own kind than are the people of the light. I tell you, use worldly wealth to gain friends for yourselves, so that when it is gone, you will be welcomed into eternal dwellings.

What are we to make of this passage? Again this is a section of Scripture traditionally bypassed by preachers and expositors— perhaps because it's too easy to draw the wrong conclusions. These words are troubling, for it seems that Jesus is praising the man who cheated his present employer in order to gain favor with other people who might employ or befriend him.

But we don't believe this is what Jesus meant. He did not praise the steward for his dishonesty; the master did. (Everybody in this parable is a scoundrel!) We think Jesus is pointing out that the world is full of "systems" that the people of the world understand and exploit to their full advantage. (Dan learned this in his first few years in engineering. There were people who put up with "the system" of unclear rules and obscure regulations, combating it without really understanding it, but there were also people who knew how to work that same system to get their jobs done.)

Jesus often chided the people around him for being "slow to understand." In this passage he once again seems to be saying that we Christians (people of the light) do not understand how the world we live in works. Yet we *should* be able to use the world's systems for eternal advantage.

Worldly wealth has a use—not only for our benefit but also to help bring others into the kingdom. The good steward and the wise innocent will stand out as witnesses to Jesus. This will draw the resentment and mockery of some, and the admiration and inquiry of others.

Sheep in Wolves' Clothing

Some European believers in World War II understood this lesson and used their knowledge of the Nazi "system" to deliver Jews (and others) from prison and death. These heroes knew what bribes were, where best to apply them and how to tell the authorities what they wanted to know—whether or not it was strictly the truth. They knew how to obtain or create false ID papers and how to misdirect the attention of the murderous police. These were street-smart but heaven-bound people, and they were used by God to preserve and deliver the persecuted and the helpless.

The world we live in now is different from Nazi Germany only in degree, not in kind; it is filled with "systems" created with plausibly good intentions, but administered by flawed and sin-bound people. There is still injustice, hatred and prejudice. We are called, it seems, to be able to use these systems (righteous or unrighteous) for righteous means. We are *not* called to be naive—and won't be effective if we are.

Wise as Doves

We once declined to support a Christian from our area who was running for the U.S. Congress. His campaign was based largely on his fresh approach and personal integrity, and in one speech he claimed that he wouldn't know a bribe if it walked up and bit him.

"Wrong answer," commented Dan. "I want a representative who *recognizes* every bribe that comes along, no matter how subtle, but won't *take* one. This guy is too naive to deal with the power system. He won't last two days in D.C. without making a major mistake."

Being Christians does not automatically protect us from schemes and scams, from the deliberate deceits of the world. In fact, our openness and willingness to trust may make us easier targets. We have narrowly escaped entanglement in a vacuum cleaner repair scam. We have been cheated (though legally) out of money due us. We have avoided other problems by being cautious and aware. Our children know that we don't buy anything over the phone from people who call us. We demand our offers in writing, unless we have had previous dealings with the company.

Not all things are as they seem; not everyone is as he or she seems. Elizabeth had been sitting on the Mall in Washington D.C. with the kids, waiting for Dan to emerge from the depths of the Smithsonian. They were enjoying the music provided by a wandering flautist, and Elizabeth had given the kids a few coins to toss into his upturned hat.

Later the whole family was sitting in another place on the Mall, eating a snack, when a man wandered up and went into his sales pitch: "Could you help me out? I'm trying to get enough money for a sandwich. It's my birthday and I'm hungry" and so on. Dan stood up and offered to buy him a sandwich at the nearby hot dog stand. "Oh no," the man said, "They want too much for their food." (What difference did it make if Dan was paying?) The two of them discussed the matter for a few minutes, and then the man wandered away, without a sandwich or money for one. He walked a few yards away to another group of tourists and started his spiel again.

The kids wanted to know what had happened. "That man was asking for money for a sandwich," Dan explained, "but I don't think he really wanted a sandwich. I would guess, though I don't know for certain, that he would have spent the money on a bottle of alcohol or maybe on drugs. I would have given him food but not money."

"But was he lying?"

"Probably, from the way he acted when I offered him a real sandwich."

"But he seemed like a nice man."

"Yes he was—a little worn around the edges and apparently down on his luck, but polite and reasonably clean."

The kids still looked confused. "But why was that different from the man playing the flute?" they asked Elizabeth. "We put money in his hat."

"Yes, but he was working for it. He was giving away something of value—his music—and hoping that people would reward him for it. It's kind of like your father writing books and hoping people would like them enough to buy them."

Other clues to the meaning of "doves and serpents" come to us in the passages illuminating the paradox of being *in* the world but not *of* it.

From the Scriptures (including Matthew 5:14; John 1:29; 6:51; 8:12; 9:5; 15:19; 17:1-26) we gather that the elements of that paradox could be boiled down to a few simple but far-from-easy attributes:

1. The world (for now) belongs to Satan, the evil one, the "prince of the power of the air."

2. The believer has the same needs, desires and interests as those who are "in the world" but has different values and will make different choices.

3. The world has not known the Father and so does not know the Son.

4. Therefore the people *of* the world will hate and separate from the people who are *in* the world because they are "different."

But what does it mean in practice? How can we prove that our long-term values aren't tied to physical or temporal things?

No Dues for the Devil

It's one thing to hear—and even enjoy or appreciate at some level—music on the radio or TV. But it's something a bit deeper to actually internalize, reward and subsidize the same music.

Our daughter (then ten), a violinist and square-dancing fan, was with Dan in the car when they heard "The Devil Went Down to Georgia" on the radio.

"What's *that,* Dad? I like that music!"

"So do I, but I don't like what it's about."

They listened to the whole thing and then discussed it. They agreed on a number of things:

☐ It was extremely catchy music, with superb fiddle playing.

☐ It falsely glorified Satan and portrayed him as a fair-playing gambler who *dealt* for souls.

☐ It failed to indicate God and Jesus as the opposition of Satan, presented spiritual warfare as a conflict between human beings (unaided except by natural cleverness and talent) and Satan, and presumed that humans could win that battle on their own.

Dan and Jennifer finally agreed that though they would not deliberately and routinely listen to that song, they would enjoy it at considerable volume if it popped up on the radio—appreciating the music while realizing that they couldn't agree with the message. Some people might call that an unacceptable compromise, but we see it as being *in* the world (aware of it) but not *of* it (blindly celebrating the values of those around us).

We cannot avoid exposure to the world, but there is an antidote, an inoculation at hand, to bring life to these puzzlements and paradoxes.

—2—

Discerning
the Danger

*We must warn our children about three levels of
evil, beginning with our unavoidable
vulnerability as victims and ending with our
potentially destructive role as villains.*

Dan had gotten as far as *"deliver us from evil"* in the Lord's
Prayer one Sunday when he began pondering both the
meaning of the phrase and its relevance to this book.
"Deliver us from . . . what?"

What is evil? It seems to be something we could define neatly
and identify quickly, yet it is a problem which has tormented
theologians through the centuries. Repeated attempts have been
made to categorize and distinguish the kinds of evil and identify
their sources. But the traditional theologies of evil don't seem
adequate, especially when it comes to teaching our children. What
evils do we want to protect our children from, and what do we want
them to understand about evil?

There are several *kinds* of evil—and they're not so easy to tell
apart.

We fear the evil that falls upon us—the accidents, the ill-nesses, the tragedies, the sudden insults, the "twists of fate," the random acts of violence and senseless destruction. This is why we teach our children to swim, to look both ways before crossing the street, to dress warmly against the cold, to stay away from strangers, to avoid rough neighborhoods, to wear bike helmets and skateboard pads, to walk (rather than run) down the stairs. This is our first fear: we want our loved ones, especially our children, to be *safe*. Perhaps we can call this first kind of evil *calamity*—the externally imposed evil that causes us suffering (both general and specific).

The Evil of Calamity

The Bible has (shockingly) little to say about seeking protection from calamity in the general sense. Jesus seemed undisturbed when talking about "God's chosen people" who were persecuted by Pilate or killed when a building collapsed:

> Now there were some present at that time who told Jesus about the Galileans whose blood Pilate had mixed with their sacrifices. Jesus answered, "Do you think that these Galileans were worse sinners than all the other Galileans because they suffered this way? I tell you, no! But unless you repent, you too will all perish. Or those eighteen who died when the tower in Siloam fell on them—do you think they were more guilty than all the others living in Jerusalem? I tell you, no! But unless you repent, you too will all perish." (Luke 13:1-5)

He did not link their accident to their spiritual state—as his audience was hoping to hear—but instead he repeated his lesson about the man born blind (John 9). This misfortune was tied not to anyone's specific sin, but to the fallen state of the world and to God's glory. He pointed beyond the physical dangers to the spiritual dangers that would accompany their failure to repent. And he spoke bluntly of the persecution that would come to his followers:

> If the world hates you, keep in mind that it hated me first. If you

> belonged to the world, it would love you as its own. As it is, you do
> not belong to the world, but I have chosen you out of the world. That
> is why the world hates you. Remember the words I spoke to you: "No
> servant is greater than his master." If they persecuted me, they will
> persecute you also. If they obeyed my teaching, they will obey yours
> also. They will treat you this way because of my name, for they do
> not know the One who sent me. (John 15:18-21)

Calamity, in this sense, happened to Jesus. We assume that
Joseph had died by the time his ministry began. If so, Jesus was
also the head of his household and supporting Mary by his
carpentry. Splinters, warping wood and dull tools would have
been no stranger to him. And in what seemed at first to be the
end, he was betrayed, illegally tried, wrongfully convicted and
cruelly executed.

The tone of the remaining New Testament writings assumes a
background of suffering, both for Christians in particular and
people in general.

Search as we may, we can't find any Scriptures promising that
God will *never* let anything bad happen to his people. Romans 8
promises that nothing can *separate* us from the love of God—but
all those things in the list still have some power to hurt us and
even to end our lives. Calamity is either directed by God (if from
his hand), or permitted by God (if from Satan's hand).

Yet calamity does not in itself alter our relationship with God;
it can even bring us closer. Hebrews depicts calamities that befell
God's people and how they remained steadfast and were blessed:

> Others were tortured and refused to be released, so that they might
> gain a better resurrection. Some faced jeers and flogging, while still
> others were chained and put in prison. They were stoned; they were
> sawed in two; they were put to death by the sword. They went about
> in sheepskins and goatskins, destitute, persecuted and mis-
> treated—the world was not worthy of them. They wandered in
> deserts and mountains, and in caves and holes in the ground. These
> were all commended for their faith, yet none of them received what

had been promised. (Hebrews 11:35-38)

Of course the opposite response is possible, that is, a second evil.

The Evil of Seduction

There is an evil even worse than calamity: the kind of evil that arises when we yield to pressure or persuasion to commit sin. *Seduction* is a useful term for this evil (external or internal) that induces us to sin. (Note that our seduction may very well cause calamity for someone else!)

The entire book of Job is focused on such a conflict. Satan claims that external evil visited upon Job will cause him to indulge in personal evil by cursing God for the external evil. And throughout the trials, God never explains or justifies the external evil—but he does praise Job for remaining pure inside.

> Then the LORD said to Satan, "Have you considered my servant Job? There is no one on earth like him; he is blameless and upright, a man who fears God and shuns evil. And he still maintains his integrity, though you incited me against him to ruin him without any reason."
>
> "Skin for skin!" Satan replied. "A man will give all he has for his own life. But stretch out your hand and strike his flesh and bones, and he will surely curse you to your face."
>
> The LORD said to Satan, "Very well, then, he is in your hands; but you must spare his life." (Job 2:3-6)

And the result: "In all this, Job did not sin by charging God with wrongdoing" (Job 1:22).

But yielding to temptation makes us instruments of evil—no longer victims of circumstance but destroyers of good things.

One Scotch novel from the 1800s recorded a mother's admonishment to her young son, eager to be off to Edinburgh to test his freedom, his might and his manhood. Her words went something like this: "I wuid rather ye die young than be a stain and a horror on the land, and a reproach to yer mither in her auld age."

25

Calamity in itself does not separate us from God, but our sinful response does.

The Evil of Corruption

There is a third layer of evil even more insidious and infinitely more dangerous—the kind of evil that leads us to persuade others to join us in the wrongful activities we've chosen. Corruption is the evil that, having seduced us, induces us to recruit others into our sinful practices.

In Matthew 18:6-7 Jesus notes the special condemnation in store for those who caused children to "stumble" into sin:

> But if anyone causes one of these little ones who believe in me to sin, it would be better for him to have a large millstone hung around his neck and to be drowned in the depths of the sea.
>
> Woe to the world because of the things that cause people to sin! Such things must come, but woe to the man through whom they come!

And Romans 1:29-32:

> They have become filled with every kind of wickedness, evil, greed and depravity. They are full of envy, murder, strife, deceit and malice. They are gossips, slanderers, God-haters, insolent, arrogant and boastful; they invent ways of doing evil; they disobey their parents; they are senseless, faithless, heartless, ruthless. Although they know God's righteous decree that those who do such things deserve death, they not only continue to do these very things but also approve of those who practice them.

We still remember the story of Adam Walsh—the six-year-old boy who disappeared from a store. He was taken, killed and beheaded by a person or persons unknown; the details of his last hours and the resting place of his body are still dark mysteries. It's hard as parents to think that anything more horrible could happen to our child. But in scriptural, cosmic and eternal terms there actually are worse things than disappearance, dread, death, dismemberment and a nameless grave, and there are worse fates. To be consumed by such a horror is one thing; to become such a horror is worse; to induce others to join the slaughter is worst of all.

Shortly after two schoolboys shot and killed their classmates, a pastor friend was talking about the tragedy to a group of us. "What could be worse," he asked rhetorically, "than finding out that your child had been killed at school?"

Someone responded, "Finding out that your child had led the killing?"

No one cared to answer further.

God is sometimes the author of calamity—but he is *never* the author of seduction or corruption. (Remember, calamity is not sin, though it may be the result of sin and may bring about an opportunity for sin.) He may bring about calamity for several reasons: to show his power and character, to show through testing his people's character, to facilitate his judgment and wrath, to influence events or even to answer our prayers.

Evil can happen *to* us, *in* us and *through* us. The unsettling realization is that God is less concerned with what happens *to* us than what happens *in* us and *through* us.

Blinders and Filters

In order to protect against danger we have to recognize it when we see it coming. Identifying it after the fact is too late.

We knew a family whose father went through the TV guide each week and marked off the programs the children could watch. That seemed appropriate for his six-year-old, but we didn't understand why that should still be necessary for the well-behaved, obedient (and perhaps overly compliant) fourteen-year-old. It seemed that by that age any children should know which programs they were and were not permitted to watch and should be involved in the decision-making process. We wondered if this teenager would be able to handle the world when he was finally released and set free to choose his own way. Would he then go wild and sample all the stuff he'd never been allowed to even talk about?

The underlying question was whether the children in that family were able to recognize and avoid evil, but the broader question is how *any* child can be taught to recognize and avoid evil.

We can't recognize anything unless we have encountered it before, either in our own experience or as described for us by those with firsthand knowledge. Recognition comes from knowledge, and knowledge does *not* come from ignorance.

If the sun is too bright for comfortable driving, what do we do? Stay at home with the shades drawn? Put on a blindfold and try to drive anyway? No! We put on sunglasses to act as a *filter* and not a *blinder.* Filters screen out the harmful things embedded in our everyday experiences, without making the experiences impossible. Blinders, on the other hand, block out *everything*—the good and the bad shut away together, not in understanding but in denial.

We've come to some realizations:

☐ We can't avoid the world.

☐ We can't ignore the world.

☐ We can't join the world.

☐ We have to walk through the world, insulated, but not isolated.

☐ Therefore we have to face the world and understand it from God's perspective. We have to inspect what we see, perform a diagnosis, identify both the roots and the fruits of ideas and events around us.

We have found it helpful to ask whether an activity or idea is *edifying, neutral* or *worldly.*

Something that is *edifying*

☐ defines the universe and values in biblical terms

☐ affirms Jesus as Lord

☐ upholds righteous thoughts and actions

Something that is *neutral*

☐ neither affirms nor contradicts God's universe or values

☐ leaves room for Jesus as Lord

☐ upholds acceptable thoughts and actions

Something that is *worldly*

☐ defines the universe and values in nonbiblical terms

☐ denies Jesus as Lord
☐ glorifies wrong or misguided thoughts and actions

Something that is edifying or neutral can be enjoyed without much worry. Something that is worldly has to be approached with caution.

One of the computer games we've acquired for the children is Bible Baseball—a Bible trivia activity that is definitely edifying. Jennifer loves to play with stuffed animals, and Andrew enjoys building things out of Legos. These are neutral activities.

But when our children encountered the Star Wars universe, we had to provide some explanations, cautions and instructions. "This is a wonderful story," we said, "done with amazing special effects and some very heroic characters. But the Force is not God, and the universe doesn't work the way they say it does. You can enjoy it for the story, but just remember it has a lot of ideas in it that don't agree with what God tells us in the Bible."

We have had some fine discussions about the trilogy and eagerly await the next installments. In the meantime we are undisturbed by the sword fights up and down the stairs and the Death Star battle reenactments in the family room, for we are convinced both children have (with our help) used their "filters" to separate the worthwhile from the worthless.

We handled the *Titanic* movie in a similar fashion. Our daughter has been a Titanic buff since she was four years old. She discovered the ship on *Reading Rainbow* and has been fascinated with it and its tragic story ever since. Based largely on her long-time interest in the sunken liner, Jennifer (twelve) asked when the movie came out if she could go see the extravaganza. We made inquiries, read reviews and talked with friends who had seen it. Would it be appropriate? What about the "adult scenes"?

Elizabeth discussed with Jennifer some of the issues involved in the PG-13 movie. We saw that she was far more interested in the drama of the stately ocean liner itself than in the fictional characters Hollywood had placed on its decks. We talked about the adult scenes beforehand. Elizabeth, having a degree in fine arts, had worked through all the "naked people" arguments when she had to draw and paint nudes from live models throughout art school. Here was a good time to talk about the human form as art, as the ultimate challenge for an artist, as a reflection of God's creative genius and as a precious gift with which we are entrusted.

After much discussion and thought, we agreed to let Jennifer see it. Mother and daughter went, enjoyed it and later discussed the sexual and romantic aspects of it. Jennifer agreed that some of the things the characters did weren't right, but that didn't prevent her from enjoying the things that were right and feeling sorrow over the events that were both sad and tragic.

Our children will see many things in the world, whether we want them to or not, and they will, we hope, bring their questions to us, even if the questions are awkward. For example, one of our radio stations prides itself on its coverage of the local sports teams. A billboard they put up recently shows a background of bouncing basketballs, footballs, baseballs and soccer balls. The caption reads, "We've got balls!" Andrew saw the billboard while we were on our way to church and asked what it meant.

After brief reflection Dan took up the challenge. "Well, it *does* mean that they have radio coverage of all those sports, but there's another meaning that's fairly crude. A long time ago, when men did something brave or heroically reckless in battle, they would say that that man 'had balls,' meaning that he was a man's man, and that he must have an extra-large set of testicles in order to do the extraordinary and courageous things he did.

"The saying carried over to sports, and into life, where any man who did something extra bold or daring 'had balls.' But it's not a very nice thing to say, and besides, we know that bravery and boldness aren't restricted to men. So you know what it means now, but let's not say it ourselves."

Their naiveté will be scrubbed away either by gentle instruction or by the hard knocks of the world. But are kids no longer innocent because they're no longer naive?

—3—

Encouraging Innocence & Instilling Wisdom

*Childish innocence and worldly wisdom are not
enough to protect our children.
We must nurture in them new and different levels
and values of both innocence and wisdom.*

If evil is the enemy giving us the challenge, what is our response
and our defense? Again, Jesus calls us to this peculiar combination of innocence and wisdom—an admirable goal. But what
do we mean by *innocent? Wise?*

To be innocent is to be "free of sin" or "without penalty." But at
least three kinds of innocence come to mind.

The Innocence of Ignorance

The small child is capable of only the small sins of uninformed
selfishness. Infants aren't embezzlers, for they are ignorant of the
existence of money—it wouldn't be important to them anyway.
Children don't learn about the existence and possibility of some
sins until they hear it from their friends or see it depicted on TV.

And learn they will, regardless of what we do to protect them.
The world is more than ready to inform and corrupt them. The

human bent is toward sin and not away from it, and their own hearts will instruct them in the "ways of wickedness."

Ignorance is a condition that should be preserved as long as necessary but can only be preserved for a limited time. Once the innocence of ignorance is gone, what is left? Are we ruined forever, with no hope of innocence ever again? To answer that, we must look at another transient (and misleading) level of innocence.

The Innocence of Circumstance

The man who routinely stops off at the "gentlemen's club" on his way home after work to hoist a few brews (and eye the women) may skip a day now and then—not because he changes his mind about the nature of his actions but because he's too tired to be interested, he doesn't have enough cash or the playoffs are on the tube at home.

This may be innocence, technically, but it is a very inferior sort of innocence. It says much about the man's interests but little (positive) about his character. There is temptation, but it is blunted by circumstances and needs little effort to resist.

But honestly, and sadly, much of our own Christian "obedience" and "goodness" falls into this category. We avoid sin not by being wise and strong and obedient but by not being particularly interested in the temptation—either at all or under the specific circumstances.

Neither intoxication (by drugs or alcohol) nor smoking is a problem in our family. We have no difficulties resisting a smoke or declining of more than our twice-a-year glass of wine. Our abstinence is as much the product of common sense as it is a moral choice. We've seen the destructive effects of indulgence and aren't willing to pay the price for the vice. We understand from Scripture that the body is the temple of the Holy Spirit, which only reinforces the decision we've already made. But that's only an innocence by default. We're still choosing our own way through life based on what appeals to us and not necessarily what's right or even what's good for us.

Some sins aren't of interest to us because of who we are. We can't take much credit for being "holy" in regard to things that don't tempt us. Some sins we can "take" or "leave," and our choice is largely determined by what's happening around us and inside us. We don't fail because we're not seriously tempted. Perhaps there is a hint of this in Hebrews 12:4: "In your struggle against sin, you have not yet resisted to the point of shedding your blood." Other sins we can't seem to stay away from and are our habitual points of failure. Yet we *are* called to recognize and resist them all.

Is anything left once we have lost our ignorance and realized that circumstantial evidence is not enough?

The Innocence of Choice

Jesus wasn't naive. He knew what was in the hearts of human beings—and "would not entrust himself to them" (John 2:24). However, sometimes his watchers questioned his understanding: "When the Pharisee who had invited him saw this, he said to himself, 'If this man were a prophet, he would know who is touching him and what kind of woman she is—that she is a sinner'" (Luke 7:39).

Jesus knew. He understood prostitution and prostitutes, as well as wine and wine-bibbers, taxes and tax collectors, food and gluttons. But even knowing, he was without sin, for he did not participate.

Here is our model for the highest level of innocence—the One who saw all that was around him, who understood it all for what it was and yet refused to participate in anything unrighteous. Had he not had this clarity of vision and strength of purpose combined, the temptations he suffered in the wilderness would have undone him, for they were subtle rather than blatant, misleading rather than offensive, attractive rather than repulsive, and even reasonable rather than argumentative.

He saw all these things clearly, and yet turned away.

But if this is the level of innocence to which we are called, what kind of wisdom should go with it? Again, three levels come to mind.

The Wisdom of Personal Experience

Dan is frequently called on to fix personal computers—at work, in our home and for other people. He usually succeeds and frequently amazes people with his seemingly casual wizardry. But most of his skill comes from personal experience—from having made the same mistake before and recognizing it when it comes around again as someone else's worry. "I've seen this before!" he says. "I did this once too!" he concludes as he exterminates the problem. "And this is how I fixed it then."

On one occasion Dan and Andrew were sitting in the back of his Jeep at an airshow watching the airplanes, and Andrew decided he wanted something from the front seat. He jumped up, hurdled the seat and promptly bashed his head on the dome light assembly. After holding his head and moaning for a moment, he grabbed what he wanted from the seat, turned, started back . . . and collided with the dome light again. He collapsed on the tailgate of the Jeep, his arms clamped around his head. Dan looked over at him and commented, "Slow learner today, are we?"

Andrew laughs about it now, but he has not whacked his head on the dome light a third time.

The Wisdom of Learning from Others

There are easier ways to learn lessons. We can observe the mistakes of other people and listen to the advice of others who have already passed the forks in the road we have yet to reach.

When Dan goes to the automobile junkyard in search of parts for our cars, one or both of the children go with him. Andrew was at his side one day when they stopped to inspect a car that had been mangled in a spectacular wreck. Andrew noticed the deployed airbag and asked if it had saved the driver.

"Apparently so," said Dan. "There's no blood on it, and it doesn't look like the driver had to be cut out. But look over on this side. It looks like the passenger went through the windshield." The glass was crazed and shattered, and there was a person-sized hole with dark and ugly stains around the edges. "Think you want to ride without your seat belt on the way home?"

"No thanks, Dad." He thought for a while. "Were they drunk?"

"There's no way to tell from here," Dan replied. "But this kind of accident happens so much more easily when the driver has been drinking."

Andrew didn't respond to that, but the lesson surely sank in.

One day when a video shut off, the TV cut to an episode of *Cops*—the actual-footage show about life on the police forces around the nation. The kids wanted to watch a few minutes, and we joined them.

They were entranced, and the program eventually became a popular part of their permitted viewing. We judged it a good way to give the kids a look at the gritty part of life without having to immerse them in it personally. They enjoyed as they watched, and they learned as they enjoyed: act like this and wind up face down on the sidewalk in handcuffs with all the neighbors staring. (As "The Shadow" said, "The weed of crime bears bitter fruit.")

Older people are revered in Scripture, often rightly so, for they have lived long enough to make all the common mistakes or see them committed by others. Listening to the experiences of our elders is invaluable in maintaining innocence. It's no coincidence that Proverbs is filled with phrases like "heed my words," "spurn not my advice" and "hear this counsel." (As an older friend pointed out to us, "If it doesn't kill you, you can learn from it!" Another wise man said, "Good judgment comes from experience. Experience comes from bad judgment.")

The Wisdom That Comes from Above

We can, if we will, learn from supernatural experiences, guidance from above and spiritual discernment. We may come to a point where an action or choice lies before us and we have little to go on in making our decision. We have no personal experience that would direct our action, and we have no advice from others. Yet we may hear a "still, small voice" inside which says yes or no. And we ignore this voice at our peril, for it is often the voice of God bestowing direct heavenly wisdom.

Here is the highest wisdom—the wisdom that is beyond the wisdom of the world—wisdom that nonbelievers may not acknowledge or may even deride.

Childish innocence isn't enough. The wisdom of the world isn't enough.

We're called to more than that. To be *innocent as doves,* intelligent, informed, alert, aware, but harmless and without blame. And to be *wise as serpents,* understanding the wiles of the world and the systems around us, both to see and avoid evil and to be God's people in those systems to accomplish his purposes.

—4—

Personalities &
Personhood

*Children are individuals from the start and must
be reminded of the deliberate uniqueness
of their personalities as well as their value in the
eyes of God and their parents.*

Each of our children is a different person.

Some of the differences were apparent immediately. (Jennifer arrived in the world wide-eyed and alert, lifting her head up in the delivery room to look around. Andrew had a less pleasant time and made the transition from womb to world with a scowl. But Jennifer had colic and slept poorly, while Andrew usually blessed us all with regular nightly sleep.)

Some of the differences became apparent later. (We have one actress and one comedian. Jennifer learns by hearing explanations, while Andrew learns by doing.)

Other differences will appear as the years pass. (We can't imagine them having similar careers. Jennifer wants to be a dolphin trainer or animal handler, while Andrew seems destined for a technical career featuring fast machinery and high explosives.)

Jesus was the most *individual* individual of all time, and if he had a secret that undergirded his self-image, his sense of purpose and his confidence, it was that he knew where he had come from, he knew what he was and he knew where he was going.

We can pass some of this on to our children, for we as parents
☐ know where our kids came from
☐ know more or less who they are now
☐ can make educated and informed guesses about their future, pointing to both human probabilities and the promises of the all-knowing God

The hope is that all three parts can be discussed openly and easily.

We Talk About Their Past

We talk about their ancestors (including us), sharing stories of those days we may or may not remember ourselves, stories that go with photographs we've accumulated in a series of scrapbooks.

A family friend encouraged Elizabeth to keep a diary of her thoughts, feelings and observations throughout her pregnancy and the early years of each child's life. She promised it would be a precious document and we would all value it in years to come.

Elizabeth did and found her friend to be right in more ways than either of them knew. Elizabeth now has two diary volumes for each child. In them lie the silly details of the funny little things they did, prayers she prayed for them, her observations of their growth and development, and her personal expression of frustration with her lack of understanding of their needs. And of course, they are loaded with little love letters to the children.

Elizabeth had planned to share the diaries with the children when they got into their teens and were struggling with self-image, self-confidence, overly strict parents and the struggles of being a teenager. But one day, when Jennifer was about eleven and clearly experiencing some preadolescent fears, Elizabeth knew it was the moment to share at least one thing from her diary. She read to her a section from when she was quite little about some funny little thing she had done. She smiled; encouraged, Elizabeth read a little more. Our daughter was clearly enjoying this revelation of who she was before she could remember, but Elizabeth stopped after sharing just a few entries, to save more for another day. Jennifer loved it and kept asking to hear more.

So now Elizabeth reads pieces of the diaries to the children at different times, always for the purpose of demonstrating to them how much they are loved, how much we have enjoyed them, how much they have been prayed for, and how God is directing their lives and caring for them. Doing so is like bandaging up a sore spot, massaging a stiff back, smoothing ruffled feathers and, of course, giving a big warm hug.

Andrew loves to hear about his first complete sentence:

(At fourteen months) *Yesterday I was sitting in the family room on the couch with Andrew when Dan walked through. In a few seconds Andrew started to get down off the couch, and said, "Go see Daddy." I think that was Andrew's first documentable sentence.*

This one always gets howls of laughter from Jennifer:

(At three years) *A few days ago Dan was getting ready to take you out, and asked you to go up to your room to get your thermos. You looked at him as if to say, "Are you sure that's what you want?" He hurried you along, and off you went. A few minutes later you called from the top of the stairs, saying, "Help, Daddy. It's stuck!" Dan wondered what could have happened to get a little thermos stuck, but you had been banging around in your room, so he went to help. He got up there and you were trying to haul the heat register cover out of the floor in the corner of your room. Daddy laughed because he realized that you thought he had asked you to bring him* the furnace, *not your* thermos.

"Tell me again about when I was little!" We smile inside, because to us they are *still* little—but in their own eyes they're so much bigger now!

Elizabeth has maintained a list of their expanding vocabulary, dated, with the phonetic sounds (actual spelling uncertain) and the apparent definitions:

(Jennifer at eighteen months) *I'm not sure what you're saying, but it seems to mean "Do it again." You say "dee-dee-dee" when you enjoy something we do, and when we do it, you seem satisfied. I guess it means "Please do it again."*

Andrew giggles when told of some of his first experiments in mathematics:

(At twenty-six months) *3-4-9, you say, 3-4-9. I suppose you've heard Jennifer counting and are copying what appears to you to be a very exciting activity. You use other numbers too, 17-18-19, but always come back to good old 3-4-9. (At least they're in the right order.)*

And we remind them of things they know but may have forgotten momentarily:

(Jennifer at six) *Tonight as I tucked you into bed you said, "I know I'm the most beautifullest little girl in the whole world." And I said, "Oh? Who said so?" "I did," was the reply. Then I asked you what made you so beautiful. You said, "Because I'm nice to people," and when I asked if there was anything else you said, "God." I was pleased that you didn't say "pretty clothes," or "my hair and eyes," or anything like that. You seem to realize that beauty isn't something you see in the mirror on the wall—it is seen rather in the mirror of other people's hearts.*

(Andrew at five) *You love Calvin and Hobbes. You pore over it, read the words, and giggle and laugh. But you are really learning a lot about reading too. Your daddy picked up a lot of his first reading with a comic strip, too—Pogo! Like father, like son. We have had to explain that certain "Calvinisms" are not appropriate, will not be tolerated and are considered very heinous crimes—like nailing tacks into the coffee table, taking up the floorboards in your room or burying your mother's jewelry box in the backyard. You know that if we see your behavior beginning to reflect Calvin's negative behavior, we'll confiscate the books for a week or two.*

We Talk About Who They Are Now and How We See Them

We have tried to distinguish for them the difference between *utility* and *value*. We don't have to look very far for an example. Our house harbors a number of cats, who seem to spend most of their time curled up in a warm corner somewhere sleeping so hard and so long (and often in unnatural postures) that we have to check periodically for a pulse or whisker twitch to verify they're still alive. "You useless cat!" we exclaim as we stroke them. And they are useless at that point, but not worthless. Utility, their ability to pull their own weight and return a financial or tangible benefit to the family, is not an issue. (And we talk about how much fun God must have doing all the "pinstriping" in the fur on the cats' faces, even though the camouflage isn't required for lurking around the house.)

In the same vein, a friend-become-new-dad recently commented, "Babies are useless, but aren't they wonderful?"

Utility isn't the issue with children either. Therefore we talk about their current capabilities:

☐ "You're a good runner!"

☐ "You certainly have a way with animals!"

We even talk about their shortcomings:

☐ "You let your mind wander too far during school."

But we make sure they know that they can fail without being failures; that they can do stupid things without being stupid.

We have given them additional "names" at appropriate times. Jennifer has been known, at various times, as

☐ She Who Talks Like the Wind

☐ Nurturer of Small (and Large) Animals

☐ Player of Discarded Violins

☐ Cat Whisperer

Andrew has been called, in different circumstances,

☐ Captain Zoom

☐ Threeblade the Fierce

☐ Gadgeteer (or, He Who Bears Tools)

☐ Wielder of Weapons (small, thermonuclear devices preferred)

Naming isn't only cute, amusing or affectionate; naming can be a very powerful way to enable children for their future—or handicap them for life. Parents who call their children names like "idiot" or "clumsy oaf" may be fostering a self-fulfilling prophecy. (Sticks and stones may hurt our bones, but names can cut much deeper.)

Names should be used to bless and encourage our children—to point them toward the man or woman God is designing them to be. As we chose names for our children when they were born, we considered not only the acronym of their initials and the way the name's syllables sounded together but also the definition of each name. We wanted their life names to mean something they would be proud of, something they could aspire to, taking comfort in the fact that we were confident that they could be those things through the grace of God. Therefore we have Jennifer Elise ("fair lady, consecrated to God") and Andrew Stuart ("manly, dependable steward").

We Talk About Their Futures

It's important to talk about the future, not because we're all-knowing but because in many ways their future is our past, and some of their fears can be removed or reduced by predictions and promises.

We found that Jennifer's early years were much easier if we kept her informed about the anticipated events of the next half-hour or so. "When this video is over, we'll give you a bath, and then we'll have supper." When the time for the transition came, she was expecting it and was more or less ready for the ride. We still give the children ten-minute warnings for traumatic events like coming in from the yard for supper or finishing their reading before "lights out."

That's short-term, but the long-term predictions are no less helpful, as we talk about their changing feelings and needs:

"Someday you'll both meet people of the opposite sex who will make you feel all funny and happy inside, and that's normal. And someday you'll meet one you'll want to stay with forever, and that's normal, too. We'll try to help you pick the right one."

"Someday you may think that we are boring old people you don't want to hang out with anymore, and you'll have ideas about the world that are different from ours."

"Someday you won't want to live with us anymore." (Of course they don't believe us; they just can't imagine not living with us.)

"And someday you'll look back on these days we're living right now, and with a little catch in your throat, you'll realize that these days are the 'good old days' for you, when your life was pretty straightforward and simple."

"But when all these things change, God will still be taking care of you. We don't know what his plans for you are, but they must be pretty special."

These things will happen, and we hope they will remember that they were told so. We hope the forewarning will be a comfort and not an irritation.

—5—

Life, Law & Order

*A child's sense of hope and order comes
from the structure and discipline of the home
and shapes lifelong perceptions
and expectations.*

We acknowledge God's sovereignty in our house, but we also establish ourselves (the parents) as the local and immediate authorities, based on the biblical patterns given to us.

From the first, our household has been run as a "benevolent dictatorship." That is, the wishes of the children are solicited, listened to and considered, but our word is the decision to be followed. Our children have seen from the first that structure and order are the rule, with a hierarchy to be considered. We issue instructions and are under instructions ourselves. Much of our effort goes into establishing boundaries and discipline, and maintaining law and order through what we have come to call "threats and promises."

Our first task of discipline was to teach our children to respect authority. If they rebel against us at the age of three and are not brought into line, later on they will resist their school teacher, Cub Scout leader, school principal and eventually their boss, the police or God himself.

We followed the lead of Ross Campbell, who teaches that punishing by spanking should be reserved for when a child is clearly challenging authority. That attitude must be changed immediately. (The child must, however, be given the freedom to ask polite, appropriate questions.)

Yes, we spanked our children—with our hands only and only on their bottoms—but only after a warning and never in hot anger. Yet because we spanked them when necessary when they were young, they quickly progressed to the point that we seldom needed to resort to such measures.

Discipline, to us, meant not that we were abusive, inflexible and quick to anger but that we established expectations, limits and penalties ahead of time—and then followed up on our threats. We learned not to set penalties we weren't prepared to enforce, and the children learned that we meant business about the penalties we did set in place.

When they were young, we simply stated the rules, giving the reason "Because Mommy (or Daddy) said so." And that's all we expected them to deal with at that point. But as soon as they were able to begin to reason, we began explaining the rules, proving (we hoped) that there was a biblical or logical reason behind the rule. We usually add that although we cannot force them to obey the rule, we can make them wish they had!

We have found that when rules are established and explained, our children understand why they are in place and often see that the rule is there for their own protection. They tend to live with a rule more comfortably when they see it as something that helps protect them, rather than something that hinders them and arbitrarily or unfairly sets them up for punishment. Yet explanations aren't always available—from God, parents or whoever—and sometimes all they can do is go along.

At one point, in discussing Dan's right to set and reset rules, we posed the children a trick question: "If the clock says it's only 7:00 p.m., but Daddy says it's bedtime, what time is it?"

Andrew got the answer right away. "Bedtime!" he grinned.

Commands have to be understood to be obeyed, and we discovered by trial and (mostly) error that our commands needed to be clear, consistent and kind to be effective.

Clear Commands

Andrew (four) was having trouble getting his boots on, though they had fit him quite well the week before. When Elizabeth came to help him, she noticed that he had on an extra pair of socks. Peeling off the top ones, she realized there were even more underneath that—a total of four pairs of socks.

"Why do you have so many socks on?" she asked him, somewhat exasperated.

"Well, you tell me every morning to put on a clean pair of socks," he said defensively.

Elizabeth had to laugh: she hadn't specifically told him to take off the dirty ones first.

In a related incident she was preparing him for a bath after a day in the dirt at the park, and told him, "Just put all your clothes in the wash." A few minutes later she caught him doing exactly that—emptying all the clothes out of his dresser drawers and putting them in the hamper.

At four he didn't understand what was implied beyond the exact words of the instructions. It's one thing to give commands that can be understood; it is more difficult to give commands that can't be misunderstood.

Consistent Commands

If we're not careful, the kids can get different orders from each parent. The effects of such confusion can cut both ways: either the children wind up trying to follow conflicting instructions, or they snatch the luxury of picking the priorities they like best.

Dan has occasionally sent Jennifer downstairs to finish her music practice, not realizing that she had come upstairs after Elizabeth told her to finish cleaning her room. Crossed wires of that nature aren't fair to the children.

On the other hand, the young ones occasionally have the opportunity to ask us separately for permission to do something—and to play us against each other if we don't give the same answers. That isn't fair to us, for it strains our harmony and puts us in the position of choosing which priorities are followed.

The only cure we've found so far is communication—making sure both of us as parents are on the same page of the instruction book regarding not only the operating rules but also current needs, responsibilities and freedoms. (If an existing plan is changed by one spouse, the other spouse needs to be told promptly.)

Kind Commands

Humor, exaggeration and mild irony go farther than coldness or anger, though occasional bluntness with a trace of added volume isn't always misplaced.

Elizabeth entered the kitchen one morning, and the first thing she said to Jennifer was "Honey, I see you didn't feed the cats. Remember, first one down in the morning gets the honor." Two minutes later she was pointing out something else left undone and saw the slump in Jennifer's shoulders. It hit Elizabeth then that she was failing as a mother at that moment—being more concerned about the daily schedule than she was about Jennifer's feelings. Yes, our daughter had failed to do the things that she knew were her responsibility, but Elizabeth could have been gentler in handling the correction. She acknowledged that she was being selfish, pointing out Jennifer's failures to justify her own irritability. Elizabeth apologized, hugged Jennifer and told her that she was proud of the things she *had* remembered to do. She might have forgotten something, but it was Elizabeth's responsibility to control her feelings. The mother, after all, was supposed to be the adult in this situation.

We often recalled that supposition when the children were babies. We would be frustrated with their crying or fussing and would have to remind ourselves that *we* were the adults here and it was our job—not the child's—to come up with a workable solution to the problem.

Now that the children are a bit older, Dan has been known to survey the clutter around the kids in the living room and remark, "You know, the Big Daddy of the house will be coming through here in a few minutes, and it would probably be a very good thing if he didn't find all this wreckage in the way." Then he leaves, knowing that the hint has been delivered gently, relieved that he doesn't have to resort to "Clean up this room!" to get results.

Threats and Promises

Lines are drawn with prohibitions and threats, while motivation is sustained through promises. We realized—the hard way, as usual—that we have to make good on our promises as well as our threats. It's a two-sided action: we try to live up to our promises, but we also try to limit our promises.

If the kids ask if we can go somewhere or do something, and there is no definite time attached to it or it's considerably in the future, we generally say, "We might—no promises." This serves notice that (1) it sounds interesting, (2) we don't object to it in principle, (3) it's not of highest priority, (4) we'll try to remember the request at the appropriate time, (5) we'll make a definite decision at a later date, and (6) don't build all your hopes on it, because it might not happen after all.

If it doesn't sound like a good idea or a feasible project the answer is "I doubt it." This indicates that (1) it doesn't sound like a great idea, (2) but we'll talk about it in more depth at another time, yet (3) we haven't flat-out said no.

We do say no (not subtle or negotiable), but wherever possible we say yes to their participation in Christian or neutral activities.

(If we have any regrets, it's that we didn't say yes more often to their simple and childlike requests. Too many times we have been tired and distracted, with no resources of patience or energy to agree to their requests for snuggles, bike rides or game-playing. Yet we could, if we had refocused on the children instead of urgent-but-not-important events, have made some time for their immediate needs.)

There is a danger, however, to saying yes without thinking it through. We'd rather say maybe and deliver a pleasant surprise later than say yes and bring about disappointment when the realities of life intervene. We need to show that we ourselves are responsible for (1) making decisions, (2) keeping promises (or at least specifying "no promises" up front) and (3) accepting consequences without undue complaint.

We have spent a fair bit of time disciplining (training, directing, teaching) our children; we have spent very little time punishing them. Many people tell us we have good kids. They *are* good kids, but it's as much a part of the love, care and training they have received as it may be the genes they were assigned.

In general, the rules have worked, yet we don't claim to be infallible. We apologize when appropriate and modify or bend the rules when we deem it necessary. Still, the rules won't be effective unless the threats that accompany disobedience are backed up and carried out.

One of our rules has been "No toys at the dinner table." Unfortunately for Andrew, almost anything can turn into a toy when you're an inquisitive boy and your father has taught you all his bad engineering habits. One evening Andrew was distracted from his baked chicken by the prospect of building a pyramid with the jelly jars and spare silverware.

"That, in effect, is a toy at the table," Dan warned.

"I know," said Andrew and continued his architectural pursuits.

Dan reached out with his fork and whacked him lightly across the knuckles.

"Hey!" hollered Andrew, drawing his hand back in a hurry. He was more surprised than stung.

"We don't play at the dinner table," Dan said. "I didn't hurt you, but I did want to get your attention. Did I?"

Andrew nodded, still big-eyed, but starting to smile.

"At least I didn't use the side with the points on it," Dan added with a twinkle in his eye.

Once was enough. Now whenever Andrew starts rearranging things on the table, Dan merely has to wave his fork meaningfully in the air. Andrew gets the point, giggles and returns his attention to his food.

Another incident at the dinner table has passed into family legend. A few years ago, after the children had graduated from high chairs and booster seats, we discovered we could not keep them still in their seats long enough to eat their meals. They would interrupt their feeding activities to chase or pet cats, look out the window at the birds or dash into the other room to investigate a noise. Several rounds of requests did little to improve the situation, until finally Dan told them, "The next time you get up without being excused, I will strap you into your chairs with seat belts!" The kids giggled, knowing that seat belts aren't standard equipment on kitchen chairs.

"I may kid you a lot about some things," Dan continued, "but *I ain't foolin'* now. If you get up again, you'll have to wear seat belts for the rest of the meal."

The inevitable happened. Both children forgot the unlikely (though clear) threat and soon were dancing around the kitchen. Dan stood up quietly, folded his napkin and went out to the back porch, where he had stashed some parts he was using to restore his beloved old car. He returned with two authentic automotive seat belts and belted both kids into their chairs. They were astonished but couldn't complain on the grounds they hadn't been warned.

The belts stayed on the chairs for a week or so, but we didn't need to actually use them again. Their presence was enough; even now, the words "We ain't foolin'!" serve as stark reminders that a given threat has not been uttered in jest.

Discipline isn't punishment; it's establishing that law and order is there for the common good and will be enforced when necessary.

Proverbs 22:15 reminds us that "folly is bound up in the heart of a child, but the rod of discipline will remove it far from him"—not merely a rod but a rod of *discipline.* This follows Proverbs 19:18, which tells us, "Discipline your son, for in that there is hope." Hope for what? Our hope is that our children will become adults who can control their thoughts, tongues and actions. This will save them from many pains, both spiritual and physical.

Children raised without discipline will not have learned wisdom at a young age, when it is easiest to learn. Either they will have to learn discipline as an adult—the hard way—or they will not be a disciplined adult and probably will not be able to raise disciplined children of their own.

—6—

The Truth of Consequences

Children must learn to bear the consequences
of their actions. Actions—good and bad—
have consequences—also good and bad.
There are physical laws in the universe,
and moral ones as well.
They will not change for our convenience,
and we ignore them at our peril.

We had some principles in mind when we began raising our family; we've added several since then and clarified some that we already had. One of the first was this: *Children must learn to bear the consequences of their actions.*

When they were rugrats, we had to watch our kids and continually estimate the amount of danger they could get into. If they were heading for something dangerous, we did one of two things: we either removed the danger or moved the explorer elsewhere.

As they grew older, we could tell them "Don't!" and then inform them of the risks of the situation. But there eventually came a day when they were big enough both to understand "no" and to decide to act for themselves. Though they needed to learn the risks of disobedience, it was an unnatural act for us as parents to sit back and watch them pet the cat after being warned not to touch her "while her tail is twitching like that." They would proceed on their own course, get swatted—as we had predicted—and come crying to us with four new grooves on the back of their hand. They quickly learned that in such cases we would readily supply bandages and kisses but no sympathy. "That one was self-inflicted," Dan would say. "We told you not to do that or you'd get hurt!"

The same principle applied later to situations like Andrew trying to see how many steps he could skip coming down the stairs. "It may be fun," we said, "but you'll eventually get hurt!" It was, and he did.

A group from church was heading out into the frosty night for Christmas caroling. One of the small boys in the group refused to wear his winter coat, mittens or a hat. "Trust me," his father said, "you are going to get *cold*." But the boy stubbornly donned his favorite jean jacket and headed for the door. Dan offered his stocking cap to the father as emergency backup, but he politely declined. "No, thanks; we're in the stage now where we're trying to teach him that Mommy and Daddy are generally right and need to be listened to. I'd rather he learn a lesson than have warm ears."

If children don't learn to deal with consequences, they will run into the same problem again and again. One of Elizabeth's long-running struggles has been getting the children to pick up their toys and keep their rooms reasonably tidy. The approach she finally settled on (once they reached about five years old) was to identify the specific objects of clutter and say, "These need to be picked up. They are in the way. Please pick them up now, or in the next five minutes."

This request if ignored or forgotten results in a warning: "If these are not picked up in five more minutes, I will pick them up and put them away. And if I put them away, you won't see them again for two or three weeks."

In the early years Elizabeth did confiscate a few toys and books, and even now she finds it occasionally necessary. A similar rule applies to their rooms; if Mom has to restore law and order herself, she will do it with a garbage bag in hand, and the children's carefully hoarded "trash" will be on the endangered list. (She has only had to do that once, so far!)

Library fines grew to be a similar issue. For a long time all the children's books were checked out on our cards. When their books were misplaced and not located in time, we simply paid the fines. But then we began to recognize a pattern *and* that our children weren't learning. So we had them sign for their own cards as soon as they were old enough and launched them into a new era. They could check out as many books, and occasionally videos, as they pleased, but it was their job to keep lists of books checked out, mark the due dates on the calendar and pay any fines that were incurred.

It wasn't long before they started learning their own lessons. Andrew forfeited eight weeks' allowance when he had to pay the fines for two overdue videos. Some lessons are tough on all of us. It hurt us as parents to watch him stand there at the library counter and painstakingly add up his dimes and quarters and wrinkled dollar bills, but we were convinced it was important that he learn.

He paid and he didn't complain that it was unfair. He knew the rules; it was his mistake and his price to pay. But he also knew he wasn't in trouble with us; we hadn't yelled at him or questioned his intelligence. All we had said was "Oops! Looks like it's going to cost you. Well, we can go to the library and you can straighten it out with the librarian." The "we" in that sentence is important: although we won't rescue our children from the rightful consequences of their misdeeds, we want them to know that they are not alone.

This story, from a source no longer remembered, exemplifies the kind of support all children should have:

> A small-town teen-aged boy had been arrested for shoplifting (his first official offense, though there had been trouble within the family). His father convinced him to plead guilty, and then asked for a private audience with the judge prior to sentencing.
>
> "I don't know if I could have done anything different to help him," he told the judge, "but I think there's something I need to do now. He stole the merchandise, and he needs to understand that punishment follows crime. I don't want him to get off too lightly, but I don't want

him crushed, and I don't want him to think he's all alone. The sentence I'm asking for is this: three weekends in the local jail, and I'll serve the time with him."

The judge replied, "I was going to let him off with a fine and probation, but I think I see what you're trying to do. Two weekends, then, for the two of you, and probation for him."

As far as I know, the story had a happy ending. The boy got a sobering taste of the power of the law and the reality of jail, he and his father had lots of time to talk and renew their relationship, and the boy was reminded that even though he couldn't escape the earthly consequences of his behavior, his father was with him all the way.

It's not only the children who have to pay the price of consequences of their behavior. Parenting has its pains as well as its joys. So too for God: God took delight in creating us and was willing to set us free to follow our own wills. That was probably one of the hardest things he ever did, but it was one way he has shown his love for us. He has had to live with the consequences of his children's behavior and choices. He has gone through all the pain and agony we have inflicted on him as we have chosen not to follow his wisdom.

Our children learn in school that "every action has an equal and opposite reaction." They learn at home that every action also has a consequence—good, bad or trivial. Our privilege as Christians is to separate earthly consequences from eternal consequences. Penalties may have to be paid, but there is always a place for forgiveness and the continuation of relationships.

The parent of an adult child who had made some very poor choices commented to us that although they did not approve of the child's choices, they continues to love and support their grown child, and they always will, no matter what. This was not spoken in a biblical sense, but it sounds a lot like what God has been saying to us for thousands of years.

—7—

Responsibility & Freedom

*Children should be given as much responsibility
and freedom as they can handle.
Freedom is earned by the demonstration of
responsibility. They must go
together—responsibility without freedom
is slavery, while freedom without
responsibility is lawlessness and destruction.*

A s children grow, their world gets bigger, and so, quite properly, should the part of life's load they carry.
Children should be given as much responsibility and freedom as they can handle.

Responsibilities, like privileges, are acquired gradually. When Jennifer was seven, she desperately wanted to take horseback riding lessons, and one of her gifts that Christmas was money for that purpose. A family friend agreed to teach her for a fee suitable to a seven-year-old's budget, and Jennifer eagerly awaited summer and the start of lessons. When the grand moment arrived, we let her handle the payments to her instructor. She had to count out the money from her piggy bank, secure it in her pocket and hand the money over at the appropriate time. We wanted her to see firsthand that the lessons did cost some money but that they were worthwhile. We wanted her involved as the money changed hands each week.

Dan's parents helped out in the area of teaching them about money as well. When they went out to eat with the children, they let the young ones hand over the cash at the counter and return the change to the proper owners.

Jennifer began her babysitting career when she was nine as a "mother's helper," hired by the neighbors to come over and play with their toddler while they remodeled the kitchen. Jennifer didn't have to shoulder the whole load of child care and house-watching that comes with unattended babysitting; she had only to play with and care for the kid and keep her safe, happy and out from underfoot in the construction zone. She didn't have to answer the phone, fix any meals or worry about calling 911 if fire broke out or burglars broke in. But she was perfectly capable of changing diapers and being a role model, play partner and leader.

That was appropriate for a nine-year-old and a good start for a more responsible career. Other helper jobs opened up for her around the neighborhood, and at twelve she started babysitting "for real" for the neighbors directly next door. It helped that our family room windows are about ten feet apart and we could look across the gap and check on her throughout the evening. Help was only a wave or a phone call away. (The first few times, when her charge went to bed, Dan went over and sat with Jennifer and kept her company until the parents arrived home. On subsequent occasions she felt secure enough to stay on her own the whole evening.) Eventually she'll be on her own as a sitter, but we want to make the transition as comfortable as possible. Her confidence will grow with each success, and so will her ability.

As they grew old enough, we assigned Jennifer to be "Our Lady of the Litter Box" and Andrew to be "The Guru of the Garbage Cans." They each are learning to do their chores basically unprompted: Jennifer keeps the cat's area sanitary and fresh, and Andrew gathers the trash every Monday night and collects the empty trash cans from the curb on Tuesday afternoon. The assignments weren't arbitrary, for Jennifer wants to work with animals, and her first assignments in formal training will be the less-than-glamorous tasks like cleaning the cages. Andrew, too, is learning that the humble tasks don't have to be degrading.

Yet it was a learning process for us as well, for we initially tried to assign these responsibilities before they were able to handle them well. We backed off after our first attempts and tried again later. Elizabeth is still struggling to teach the children to sweep the kitchen floor properly without being reminded. She didn't allow them to do it when they were little, because our broom was so much bigger than they were. But now that they're of adequate size, they don't have the habit or the practiced skill. Elizabeth has generally tended to do the housecleaning herself, finding it a faster way to an acceptable condition, but she wishes she had involved them when they were younger; it would have taken more time and effort then but less emotional energy, and would have brought greater reward now. There's no formula to apply in assigning responsibilities; the only way we could determine the proper amount of responsibility and the appropriate level of privilege was to know our children, try things and monitor the results.

All in the Family
Children become a vital part of the family when we make them partners in our lives at home. We can enlist their help with tasks while they're eager to help. If they aren't allowed to be partners in labor when they're young, they won't want to help when they're older.

(Andrew at six) *You've been helping Daddy with salvaging some old computers—cleaning them up, taking out the hard disks, etc., and today Daddy said to you, "In a minute you can help me take these downstairs." You asked, "Would you please repeat that, Daddy?" So he did. Then you asked Daddy again to repeat what he had said. He did, but added, "Andrew, haven't you heard what I've been saying, or do you not understand what I mean?" Then you responded, "I understand; it just makes me feel good to hear you say that I can help you!"*

Andrew is eager to start mowing the lawn and almost large enough now to handle the mower. Soon he will be taking on that chore solo, but this year he has been helping Dan when he can. Granted, it *can* take longer to do a job when children help, but that's part of the price of training them.

"No, turn that knob the *other* way."

"Don't mow the flowers."

Andrew was also involved with Dan in taking cans, bottles and papers to the recycling dumpster. "I'll do it," offered Andrew.

"Okay with me," Dan replied. "I'll wait here in the car. Just pitch the stuff in the proper compartments."

Andrew took Dan literally—and threw every item into the bin from ten feet away, winding up and delivering each throw like a baseball pitcher. There were lots of misses, and it took Andrew approximately twelve minutes to empty two pails of cans and plastic bottles into the dumpster. But Dan had a short nap over the steering wheel, Andrew had fun, and all was well with the world.

Family Life Makes Children Fit for Society

We seem to be afflicted with elected officials and so-called heroes who can't, or won't, say the words "I was wrong. I'm sorry." However, we can reverse that trend in our own homes.

One day a loud crash alerted us to something broken in Andrew's bedroom. Elizabeth discovered Jennifer there on her knees, picking up shards of glass from the broken light globe that had (until very recently) been part of the ceiling fan. She lifted a tear-streaked face toward Elizabeth and said, "I'm sorry. It's my fault. I was swinging this stick around and I hit it."

Elizabeth was very pleased and proud that Jennifer had freely admitted her involvement and relative level of guilt. It was, after all, an accident caused by carelessness and not an act of deliberate destruction born of rebellion or anger. But because it was the fruit of carelessness, Jennifer paid half the cost of a new globe. It was all repaired that same day, and the incident was closed.

We assume that this was the result of her having heard us say those difficult words ourselves, admitting our faults and failures. As that wise man G. K. Chesterton pointed out, it is better for rulers to *set* an example for their charges than to *make* examples of them.

What we do together with our children they will see; what they see they will learn; what they learn they will pass on.

—8—

Tackle the
Tough Ones
—at Home

*The child old enough to ask a question
is old enough to receive a straight (and
appropriate) answer.
Anything critical, controversial or
dangerous should be learned or discussed at
home. This isn't always easy,
but it is rewarding. When we recognize
maturity in our children and respond to them in
kind, we enable them to grow.*

At the risk of simplifying life beyond recognition, we realize
that our children are driven by three basic emotions—love,
fear and curiosity. There are both good and bad aspects to
this, but we are in deep trouble if we don't acknowledge the
existence and strength of these motivations.

Whatever they love, they love fiercely, unquestioningly, even
irrationally.

If they're afraid of something, they want nothing to do with it,
whether it exists in reality or only in their imagination.

Whatever they want to know, they want to know now—all of
it—to the temporary exclusion of all other things. This refrain of
"Why?" won't stop until the child is completely satisfied by knowl-

edge, distracted by something more interesting or else discouraged from asking again. (But discouragement only suppresses and diverts the curiosity; if Mom and Dad don't answer their questions, their friends at school will. And some of those answers will be wrong, misleading or dangerous.)

Our children have led us to a few realizations.

Even if the objects of their love are not worthy, their love is real. Children become irrationally attached to odd things like blankets and toys, inanimate objects that simply can't return the lavish love bestowed upon them. (At least we know that, but it can't be explained to them, and perhaps it's better not to try.)

One night Dan made the mistake of trying to talk Andrew into giving up his baby blanket. It had already passed the "worn" state and was nine-tenths of the way to complete disintegration. "Your blankie is about to fall apart," Dan said gently (as though they had never had this conversation before). "Don't you want Mommy to clean it and tuck it away while there's still something left to save?" After a few moments, Andrew bravely and silently handed over the pitiful remnant, and Dan proudly delivered it to Elizabeth as proof that their little boy was reaching a milestone.

But a few minutes later Elizabeth heard Andrew crying softly into his pillow and discovered that he wasn't quite ready after all; he had only surrendered the blanket because he thought Daddy expected him to. Of course the blanket was restored immediately with explanations, apologies and praises for his willingness to obey what he thought was a command.

Both of us decided not to mention the matter to him again, and then discovered that we didn't have to. A few days later, unprompted, Andrew brought the blanket to Elizabeth and asked her to preserve it for him. He reached the milestone all right, but on his timetable, not ours. We had underestimated the depth of his love for the soft-woven network of threads that had comforted him all the days (and mostly the nights) of his young life.

Even if the objects of their fear are not real, their fears are real.

Although Andrew (at eight) enjoyed his first video viewing of *Jurassic Park*, he had fears sparked by the movie. "I can't sleep," he whimpered. "There are dinosaurs outside my bedroom window." Though he knew in his head that dinosaurs were extinct, he was still afraid. We couldn't reason with him while the darkness surrounded us; we let him come in to our bedroom and sleep on pillows on the floor.

We talked the next day, but he spent the next night on our floor too. We didn't want to tell him, "Don't be *afraid*," because there is a place for fear, and his fear was real, though misguided. We finally convinced him, though, not to be afraid of imaginary *dinosaurs*. He spent four nights on our floor before the weight of reason and the voice of experience could quell his fears.

Even if the objects of their curiosity are inappropriate, their curiosity is real. All of this leads to some tough questions—questions we shouldn't ignore, deflect or parry with a half-answer.

Explaining that something "is bad for you" or is something "nice people don't do" may be enough to establish parameters for behavior, but it is not enough to satisfy curiosity—the drive for knowledge.

Dan was driving with the kids (six and nine) one day, and they passed a local "gentlemen's club" called Babes. Jennifer read the sign and exclaimed "Look! Is that a toy store?"

"Depends on your viewpoint," said Dan, which, of course, went utterly over their heads. He had three choices: he could ignore the question and divert their attention, tell them it simply wasn't a nice place to talk about or meet the challenge head on. He chose the last approach. "It's a place where men go to drink beer and watch women take their clothes off."

His words were met with complete and absolute silence. The children weren't embarrassed, but they were completely mystified as to why anyone would even want to do that.

We talked about it later at home, and the kids came to understand the *what* of it, even if the *why* still eluded them. The facts are not hidden from them. They won't wonder as they grow up what happens inside those odd little buildings with giant neon signs and no windows, the mysterious businesses that Christians won't talk about.

We have, I hope, defused the power of curiosity, especially the curiosity that takes on a different and darker flavor when the object is not only *mysterious* but *forbidden.*

The child old enough to ask a question is old enough to deserve a straight (and appropriate) answer.

Straight because we shouldn't lie to our kids. *Appropriate* because some answers are better and more complete than others.

How Much Is Enough?

We can under- or overestimate the level of information our child needs.

The story is told of a schoolboy who asked his mother how he was born. "The stork brought you," she said.

Next he asked his grandmother how his mother was born; the reply was "We found her under a cabbage leaf in the garden."

So he asked a similar question of his great-grandmother and received the answer "Well, my dear, we had to order your grandma from the Sears catalog!"

Pondering all these things, the boy sat down at his desk and started his school report: "There have been no normal births in our family for generations."

We can also give them too much information. When their little eyes glaze over during an explanation, we're telling them more than they want to know.

In any event, children will learn from experience that we do (or don't) answer their questions honestly. If we are reliable sources to them as little children, they will continue to come to us in their teens. But if we don't answer our children's questions, they will find someone else to answer them. And that should scare us, for the answers they will find elsewhere, by their own resources, are likely to be misleading, incomplete, wrong, dangerous or even fatal. *Anything critical, controversial or dangerous should be learned or discussed at home.*

Elizabeth was reading aloud to the kids as part of the nightly bedtime wind-down-and-go-to-sleep snuggle. This evening's choice was a *Foxtrot* comic collection, and they came upon a cartoon that involved the two younger boys debating whether the size of Miss October's "hooters" would affect the time needed to download her picture from the Internet.

Elizabeth reached the punch line and suppressed a giggle.

Andrew asked, "What are *hooters*?"

"Breasts," replied Elizabeth. "There are all kinds of slang words for parts of the human body."

"Is that a word we can use?" asked Jennifer.

"No," replied Elizabeth. "It's a rude and crude word."

Dan (in the next room) could hear two little brains tucking away all this information. He smiled, pleased at the low-key but direct way Elizabeth had handled it. No shame attached to the lesson, just a little healthy embarrassment.

Home is exactly where such interactions should take place.

We are the greatest (and the worst) examples our young kids will see, because we are the nearest and the clearest. We are their handiest source of information and should be their most reliable resource. They can't readily model in their lives what they don't see in ours; that is both our privilege and our burden. We try to tell our children not "shut up and listen" but "sit down and see."

Christianity is a lifestyle as well as a faith, and it is caught as well as taught. Proverbs 22:6 reads, "Train a child in the way he should go, and when he is old he will not turn from it." God wants our children to be trained to be in relationship with him. As parents it is our responsibility and privilege to teach this to our children. (Second Kings 17:41 tells a sad tale. It demonstrates how children follow their parents' example in worship. It tells how the people were worshiping the Lord but at the same time holding onto their idols. The verse continues with "To this day their children and grandchildren continue to do as their fathers did.") It's highly probable our children will end up following the example we set. It's vital to set a good one.

—9—

Keeping
Them Safe

*Physical and personal hazards are perhaps
the most obvious dangers in parents' eyes.
Children must be helped to be
both street-smart and safe around the
house and the neighborhood.*

F ire, traffic, sharp objects, poisons, strangers—all these are
things we must warn our children about.

Review . . .

One of our most dramatic opportunities came when the evening
news aired footage of a burning house—a fire started by children
playing with candles.

"How can a candle burn a house down?" wondered Jennifer
(eight).

"I won't burn our house down," said Dan, "but I'll show you how
it happened."

After supper Dan gathered up a pile of newspapers, an empty
cardboard box, a candle and a box of matches. He carried everything out to the back yard and had the kids drag the garden hose
over to the box.

"Shred the newspaper," he told them, "and throw it in the box." They did so.

Then he lit the candle. "Look at it," he said. "Not much light and not much heat." They put their hands near and felt the slight but intense warmth. "Do you think it would be hard to put this out?"

"No," they answered.

"That's right. I could put it out with my fingers if I had to. But watch this." Dan tossed the burning candle into the cardboard box, and in seconds the paper blazed into a four-foot flame.

"How close do you want to get to that?" Dan asked the big-eyed children.

"Not very close!"

"That's right. Suppose that was your room on fire. Could you stay in it?" They both shook their heads solemnly. "Could you fight the fire yourself? Could I even put it out with my fingers?" More solemn shakes. "No. You would get out, call for the firefighters from the neighbor's house, let the professionals do it. But most important, don't let a fire start in the first place! That's how a big fire can start with a little flame."

Then Dan turned on the hose and let the kids put the fire out. When the ashes were cool enough to poke through, Dan showed how thoroughly everything had been burned. "Complete destruction," Dan said. "Fire does this to wood, to paper and to people. We don't mess around with fire."

In this case, *show* was better than *tell*.

... and Previews

A year or two later at a neighborhood festival where local firefighters had a display, one fireman donned the full rescue gear, dropped down on his hands and knees, and showed the gathered kids what he'd look and sound like up close in the heat, smoke and darkness. "You can't see my face, can you? Or hear me very well. I even look a little bit like Darth Vader. But if you ever see me in a fire, you trust me, and come with me, because you need me to get out alive."

There are some home fires we don't want burning.

Relatives, Friends and Other Hazards

We have given our children the standard "stranger danger" lectures, but we have to realize that friends, neighbors and even relatives can pose threats of various kinds.

Friends told us of the day their three-year-old daughter said that her male preschool nursery helper at the new church they were attending had touched her between her legs. The parents weren't sure what to do. They asked their little girl if she was being held or carried when she was touched, and the child was unsure. The child had attended a "good touch/bad touch" program at her preschool, and the parents had reviewed the material with her. They prayed for wisdom to know how to deal with this situation. They didn't want to involve the authorities if it was simply an innocent touch from carrying the child. And being new at this church, they weren't sure whom to talk to and felt unprepared to approach the man himself.

The parents did talk in unspecific terms with the other nursery helpers who were present that morning, but they were unable to come to any conclusions. They asked their child one more time about being touched, and the child seemed to have forgotten. So they spoke with a Social Services representative, who asked the child a few questions. Together, they decided to let the matter drop. The parents also decided to help in the preschool for the few remaining weeks of the semester.

Later the parents asked us if we thought they did the right thing. Were other children now at risk because they hadn't pursued the issue any further? Possibly. Should they have gently confronted the man with the child's story so he would know what the child had said, and also so he'd know he would be watched? Possibly. The parents know that their child is fine, and they had approached the right authorities, but they wondered if they had missed something the Lord wanted them to do.

Another family tells of a difficult incident because it involved relatives. Every week or so they left their eighteen-month-old child with an older (and childless) cousin for two hours while Mom went shopping. The lady loved having the delightful child around, it was a nice break for Mom, and the baby seemed happy.

However, one day the mother noticed some potentially dangerous things lying around at a level accessible for the child—scissors, a nail file and toothpicks. Knowing that the child had the mobility to get to them but no smarts to know what they were or how dangerous they could be, the mother pointed these things out to the cousin and asked if they could be put away before the child visited again. The lady felt that the mother was challenging her babysitting know-how, and refused, saying that no one had the right to tell her what she could and could not have lying around her house. She concluded by claiming that no child had ever been hurt under her care.

The young parents discussed the situation and decided that they would have to tell the cousin that the child would not be able to come to visit her at her house if there were dangerous things lying around, and that if she wished to see the child she was welcome to visit their home. The cousin was furious and blamed them for "breaking up the family" over something as simple as scissors.

Naturally this was upsetting for the parents, but they believed they were doing the right thing. They prayed for wisdom, and soon they realized that they were actually being spared more difficulties in the future. They later discovered that this same lady did not expect children visiting in her home to say "please" and "thank you" and made candy available to them at any time. She also had been known to tell visiting children that they didn't have to tell their parents about having candy—it could just be "their little secret."

When the parents heard about these things they thanked God for rescuing them from more trouble in the future; however, their relationship with the cousin remained strained.

Secrets and Surprises

Our knowledge of these encounters led us to discuss with our children the difference between secrets and surprises. A surprise is sort of a temporary secret, made delightful by the knowledge that *someone* is going to have a happy but unexpected event in their life, and the plotters get to set it up and watch it happen. Surprises are appropriate for birthdays and Christmas, and organized conspiracies are great fun. A parent may be the "target," though surprises (at the age of our children) generally aren't for both parents simultaneously. Later on they may take initiative, but for now they need Mom or Dad to drive them around and help them acquire the necessary items and distract the other parent while the goodies are wrapped in a distant room.

At this age we see no need for a child to have true secrets from both parents. (There may be private faults and private confessions; not everything Jennifer has done is known to Andrew and vice versa. Jennifer has shared some things with Elizabeth that she felt reluctant to share with Dan, and Elizabeth has kept these to herself as well; similar bonds of privacy are developing between Dan and Andrew.)

Actually, it hasn't been difficult to get our children to tell us about their lives. We just have to take the time and energy to listen to the stream of words that flows around us. Their enthusiasm generally bubbles over when they're with us again after a few hours playing "on their own," and we have encouraged them to tell us all of the important stuff—even the stuff they don't think we'll be that happy to hear about.

We tell them, "You've heard other kids say, 'My parents would kill me if they found out.' Well, there's nothing you could do wrong that we would kill you for or even beat you. Punish you? Definitely, but appropriately and not in anger. Ground you? Possibly. Question your good sense? Probably. But we need to *know* if you've gotten yourself into trouble or if someone else is trying to get you into trouble. If someone invites you to do something but warns you not to tell, then it's wrong—at a minimum—probably dangerous and very possibly illegal."

Recently Jennifer came up with the next wrinkle on the topic.

"But if someone tells me a secret," she asked, "do I have to come tell you?" (Of course this is something a younger child may not think about right away.)

We kicked some possibilities around and came to a conclusive and comprehensive answer: "It depends."

"It depends on *who* told you the secret and *why*," we said. "Was it a friend just playing, or were they afraid of something? Was it your aunt who was planning a special treat for someone else, or was it an adult who wouldn't normally tell you something privately?

"It also depends on *what* the secret is. Has someone been hurt, or are they afraid of being hurt? Are they being touched inappropriately? Has someone's property been damaged or destroyed? Is there reason to think there could be some damage or theft?"

They thought about that for a moment. "But if they're our friends, they'll trust us not to tell."

"That could be a conflict," we answered, "and telling might very well damage your friendship. But *not* telling could destroy your friend. If you're not sure, tell us anyway," we continued, "and we'll go over the guidelines again and decide together. If it's an okay secret, we won't tell anybody."

We played "what if" with a variety of age-appropriate scenarios to demonstrate that this was a matter of discernment, and assured them that as they matured their ability to discern these things by themselves would sharpen.

This is a dangerous world, even for the wise and wary; before we can let them go with any peace of mind, we have to give them the information and cautions they need for safe travel.

—10—

The Company
of Fools

*The problems of finding good friends and
avoiding peer pressure go hand in hand.
Children have to learn when to say no
to their friends, when to look for new ones,
and—most important of all—
that their approval comes from God and their
parents, not from their friends.*

When Jennifer was five, we began seriously to consider
home schooling for her. Part of the reason was the
wretched quality of our public school system; part of our
motivation was wanting to keep her with us for her formative
years; another factor was the transportation problem imposed by
our forced busing regulations. Even though there was an elementary school four blocks away, Jennifer would have had to ride a
school bus for up to forty-five minutes each way to a distant school.
We most emphatically did *not* want to put our vulnerable, sweet,
trusting six-year-old daughter on a lightly supervised bus full of
kids (ranging up to age twelve) for a daily dose of peer pressure,
confrontation, conflict and unwanted worldly "education."

In our opinion, such a group of children without involved adult
oversight is a company of fools. Too many children spend the bulk

of their day with other kids precisely their own age, at the same stages of emotional, physical and intellectual development, pursuing goals without eternal value and emulating mere celebrities who aren't worthy of the title *hero*.

This has been a difficult area. Home schooling has helped but has not eliminated all the problems. We do have increased control over our children's choice of peers and the amount of time spent in group play. We have also noticed their own freedom from the tyranny of age-consciousness when playing with either the neighborhood children or other home-schoolers. Their basis for picking play partners is no longer grade level but whether the other children are interesting, fun, pleasant and compatible. We have enjoyed our children especially when, as preteens, they have spent part of an afternoon playing board games with teenagers and the other half romping on the floor with toddlers and building block towers for them to knock down. (The age spread makes it easier for the young ones to model the older ones and for the older children to care for the younger ones. And this is a better model for our lives than an artificial age-segregated situation—we *should* be modeling those who are more mature and leading those who have more lessons to learn.)

Close to Home

The easiest way to moderate their exposure to peer foolishness is to keep them close by, which means that the best place for our children to play is in our home. But we don't want to keep them captive there or prohibit them from playing elsewhere. The best alternative is to make our house a place where our kids and their friends will *want* to play. There are several factors involved in making our home an attractive place to play.

We have to provide attractive facilities. We built a fairly large playset in our backyard, complete with a spiral tube slide. The neighborhood children quickly learned that they were welcome to join our kids on it, and we realized how easily we could monitor their community activities, language and behavior. Our lawn isn't destined for "House Beautiful" competition. The yard is there to play in and on, and the grass isn't sacred. Potentially dangerous items were removed or fixed when detected, and the yard was fenced in.

Inside, we have collected some interesting toys (including board and computer games) and plenty of designated play space. There is a TV set, but it's not immediately visible in the house. The chairs and sofa in the front room are arranged so that people can see each other rather than stare at a glass-fronted box. The TV lives in the family-room cabinet behind swinging doors; we bring the tube out when we decide we want to see it, and close it away when we're done. It's there to serve us, not to demand our attention.

It isn't on much at all when the weather is decent and there are other activities available. When it is on for the children's pleasure, it is either playing an approved video or tuned to an acceptable (prenegotiated) TV show.

We have to establish a kid-friendly atmosphere. The children have the general freedom to make a temporary mess. The living room is periodically declared "Lego World" or a stuffed animal kingdom; the room belongs to that chosen activity for one or two days, and then full order is restored. We the grownups simply avoid the area and do our work elsewhere for the interval. Yes, it's a mess, but it's a joyful mess, and a temporary one. What's important is that we know where the kids are and what they're doing.

We give them space to make and display their artwork and models. Andrew wanted to build a mine in the family room, so we let him. His masterpiece featured railroad tracks with zooming ore cars, a rickety trestle and a sign at the doorway that crudely but prominently proclaimed "Warning! Mine Entrance." We stepped over the track for a few days and then put it away. (The sign stayed up for months, though, which must have had visitors wondering what dangers lay in the next room.)

We have had a picnic in the living room, in winter, and hosted a January "camp out" birthday party in the front room for six boys.

We greet our kids' visitors by name and often (with permission) include them in our errands and fun activities outside the house. We try to provide the proper level of supervision for whatever play is happening. We make sure the house rules are known and enforce them as kindly and fairly as we can. Kindness and courtesy are required, and we help our kids be good hosts.

We have to provide useful services. We try to offer food, friendship, a sympathetic ear or counseling; we stay flexible to permit other parents to drop kids off on short notice, especially in emergencies. Our neighbors know they can park their kids with us in the middle of the night if need be.

Late one recent evening the paramedics came to a neighbor's house to treat their baby, who had been injured in a fall from the bed. Dan went down to see how we could help and returned with their four-year-old daughter in tow. Jennifer, who had babysat the girl before, welcomed her into her bed, read her a story, comforted her and snuggled beside her all night. The parents spent the long night at the emergency room but didn't have to worry about their daughter. They picked her up the next day rested, fed and happy. She still talks about her sudden "adventure" with Jennifer and loves to come down and play.

Friends and Foes

Children make friends easily, whether they be good friends, best friends, occasional friends, temporary friends or lifelong friends.

We take our children to a park, and it doesn't take long before they're playing with the other kids who happen to be there. Later, when we ask what a particular child's name is, we'll hear, "I didn't ask!" said with a note of wonder, as if surprised that we thought it important.

We also encourage visits by nonneighborhood friends (usually from church or sports teams) whenever arrangements can be made.

But there is a flip-side to encouraging good friendships: discouraging unhealthy ones. Making the judgment call isn't always easy. At one point we had uncommunicative next-door neighbors who had a mentally handicapped child. He was older than our kids and much, much bigger; he was as heavy as Dan and probably as strong. He also had little social sense and few inhibitions. He yelled and screamed and shoved his siblings around when he was displeased, rang our doorbell (and ran) several times a day and generally ranged where he pleased in the neighborhood.

He always wanted to come over and play in our yard, but we couldn't trust him and didn't want him in the same yard with our kids. He didn't have a bully's temperament, but he was aggressive, with no sense of other people's needs, rights or safety. He developed a fixation for four-year-old Jennifer, yelling for her to come play every time he saw her outside and sometimes at the windows when she was inside. He once urinated on her leg through our wire fence, and Dan caught him poking at our porch screens with a broom handle.

We tried all the obvious approaches. We attempted to talk with the boy and befriend him, without mixing him in with our children; we tried to supervise the play in the back yard and intervene when the boy interfered verbally; we prayed for the boy. We attempted to work with his parents, looking for something we could do to make everyone content, but in the end we had no good solutions. Though we sympathized with their difficulties in raising a child with limited abilities, we had to ask them to keep him away from our kids and our property.

We were told in response that "Christian people don't treat neighbors like that." The relationship grew strained and frosty, but they complied with our wishes. The boy was kept indoors for a long time after that, and our children expressed their thanks to us for intervening. They were now insulated from him, though not isolated; they still glimpsed him every day and heard him frequently, shouting unintelligible words in his house. Eventually he grew out of his antisocial behavior, picked other friends his own age elsewhere, and became a young man with whom we have a guarded but congenial relationship.

Did we do the right thing? I don't know, but from where we stand we'd do the same thing over again. Allowing our children more than incidental contact with him was a risk that we dared not take, for there could have been serious consequences that could not be undone. At that point we valued the welfare of our children over our relationships with (and even our witness to) our neighbors.

A Word About Heroes

Sometimes fools and heroes aren't that easy to distinguish; it's even harder if you're a child.

We can and should help them choose their heroes. Their heroes shouldn't, in general, be their peers, or they have no new levels to rise to. We tend to choose as friends people we look up to, or people who look up to us. But are peers adequate heroes? Our peers are still too much like us to be role models in more than limited areas of accomplishment.

We, on the other hand, are available. We, the parents or primary caregivers, are their first loves and potentially their lasting loves; we can also be their first and potentially lasting heroes.

They imitate us naturally when they're young, whether we think they should or not, whether we like or dislike what they've picked up. Andrew has been Dan's "wing man" for years, delighting to go in the car with him or just hang around in the area. (The destination has always been less important than the company.) Even now, at nine, he likes to dress like Dan; if he can find similar clothing, he points it out and enjoys it.

(Andrew at three) *Yesterday I went out to collect the garbage cans once the truck had come by. You followed me out and insisted on helping. So I let you drag the plastic cans—bigger than you are— around to the side of the house. I was very proud of you; I hope you'll be this helpful in ten years!*

Six years later, he is.

—11—

Troubles of
the Tongue

*Children can control their tongues,
but they have to be shown what unacceptable
language is, what's wrong with it
and what to say instead.*

O ur children hear words and terminology that we wish
didn't exist. They hear it in the shopping malls. They see
it written on the sides of bridges we pass, and they see
some of it in print in the newspaper. They need to know what these
words mean and why it is wrong for us to use them in any context,
because God has told us to not use his name in vain and to avoid
filthy language and even foolish jest that can be misunderstood
and hurtful. Frankly, the use of any expletives and profanity
indicate that the speaker has a poor grasp of language.

Unfortunately, our children even need to know how these words
are spelled. At the age of six our son innocently spelled out a
four-letter word in a composition, but we had to point that out to
him. He was talking about his summer wardrobe of shorts and a
T-shirt; however, he left out the *r* in "shirt." The episode has since

become a family joke, with gentle humor taking the sting out of it.

Blondes and Bombers

That same year, Dan took Andrew to Dayton, Ohio, to visit the Wright-Patterson Air Force Base Museum—one of the country's best collections of historic military aircraft. They were strolling down the World War II aisle when they came to the B-24 bomber. Andrew looked up at the scantily clad redhead painted on the side of the nose, spelled out the name for himself, and then turned and asked in a clear, puzzled voice, "What's a *'Strawberry Bitch'*?"

None of the other people in the exhibit area actually turned to look, but Dan could see them pausing and straining their ears to see how old Dad was going to handle this one.

"Well," he said, "you see the painting of the woman on the nose? When the men went off to war, they left all their women behind, and often they painted pictures on the airplanes of their wives or girlfriends or movie stars or women they wished they could meet. See this one's red hair? That's called 'strawberry blonde.' *Bitch* is slang for a woman who won't behave and causes a lot of trouble—a lot like the airplanes did sometimes. It's not a nice name, and it's an insult to call a woman that."

Andrew nodded and wandered on to the next airplane. Dan had somehow found the right—and appropriate—answer. In a low-key and straightforward fashion Andrew had acquired a new vocabulary word and its main meaning (though he will become aware of more nuances later), and he also learned it's not a word he's supposed to use again. (He was later taught the less common use of the word as it applies to breeding dogs.) He also realized that Dad won't go through the roof if he accidentally asks about a bad word.

He exercised that freedom several years later after a soccer game in which his team had been drilled, creamed, stomped, mangled and left for roadkill on the playing field.

"Boy," he said as he crawled into Dan's car, "we sucked today." Dan could see him watching out of the corner of his eye for a reaction to a phrase he had heard on the field but not around our house.

"That's more or less true," Dan answered, "but I'd rather you didn't use that expression. I know a lot of people do say it, but it has several meanings besides doing poorly, and one of them's a sexual slang word that's not appropriate."

Andrew nodded.

"So please find another description," Dan continued. "If you want to say that your team smelled, stumbled around, played like idiots or just plain stank today, I won't disagree with you. You all looked pretty disorganized out there."

Andrew grinned, and the conversation drifted on to other things.

Again, a painless lesson made possible by a calm and reasonable reaction.

After seeing *Jurassic Park: The Lost World* Jennifer expressed interest in reading the book. Dan dug a copy out of his bottomless pile of books and handed it to Jennifer, having forgotten by that time that the text was sprinkled with the F-word.

He discovered his mistake a few weeks later when he picked it up and started rereading it himself.

"Jennifer," he asked her in her room that night, "do you know what this word means?"

She looked at the word he was pointing at and said, "No. I couldn't figure it out."

"Well, it's a very ugly word, and I apologize because I forgot it was in there." He pronounced it for her. "You may have heard it elsewhere and not recognized it. It has a couple of different meanings. It can be a nasty way to refer to the act of sex, or it can be a term of abuse, insult, disgust and hatred. I hear people use it a lot at work—maybe so much that I didn't even notice it when I read the book the first time. I guess I wasn't paying very close attention, was I?"

They discussed it a bit more, and Jennifer seemed relieved rather than upset by the explanation. "I know what it means now, and I won't say it. I promise."

(Elizabeth was pleased to hear about that discussion, for she had had a different experience as a child. She had logically called her younger sister a "bugger" because she was bugging her; she was smacked and yelled at for using the word but was not told what it meant or what was wrong with it.)

Other people carry bad language into our house with them.

A young neighborhood friend of Jennifer's used to abuse God's name frequently. Elizabeth heard this from the other room, sighed and prayed for wisdom how to deal with this. She didn't want to criticize the child, because she had never been taught otherwise. She learned it from her parents! But we did not want this in our home, nor did we want our daughter getting used to hearing it.

So Elizabeth gently explained to the child that when she used God's name like this (when she wasn't addressing him, or talking about him to someone else), it bothered us because God is someone we know and love. So she asked her to try not to say that when she was at our house or playing with Jennifer. She very nicely complied and has continued to try to avoid this when around us.

Our children are going to hear bad language. We cannot stop up their ears every time profanity or filth pours out of someone's mouth. We don't intentionally expose them to it, but the profitable side is that we can equip them to react to it and then deal with it. We love their sensitivity. They wince and turn to look at us when they hear rough words in public or in a video, and we share a look of understanding.

We have pointed out to the children that it's interesting that it is only God's name and the name of Jesus Christ that are used in vain. Funny thing—it's not the name of Muhammad or Buddha. That goes to show that the name that we love, even when used lightly, carries a weight, a significance even to those who seem not to care. The children smile at this. They understand, and that comforts us as we see them walk about in this world.

Unfortunately, troubles of the tongue aren't limited to "plumbing words," sexual references and profanity. There are also problems such as insults, lies, babbling and inappropriate silliness to deal with.

We usually interfere when we overhear conversations between them that sounds harsh and unloving. Clarifications are requested, misunderstandings are straightened out, apologies are traded, softer words are substituted, and the incident is dropped. Once, drawn in by the not-too-pleasant tone in the children's voices, Dan intervened in a budding argument. He was about to reprimand them when he heard exactly what they were saying:

"Would you *please* stop being such a pest!"

"I would appreciate it *very much* if you would just leave my things alone!"

Dan burst into laughter and said, "I have to give you this much credit: at least you're snarling at each other politely!"

Sometimes, especially at the dinner table after they've both unloaded a torrent of bulletins, anecdotes and updates about their day's activities, we say, "Let's have a few moments of quiet from you guys so we two adults can talk for a bit. The 'cone of silence' is now descending over your heads." Dan sets a kitchen timer for ten minutes or so, and the children are expected to eat and listen quietly as we talk. It's not *punishment*—no one is mad at them— but it is good *discipline,* and it helps them see that the needs of our marriage sometimes supersede their desire to talk.

When the timer dings, they can start participating in the conversation again; by that time they've usually eaten most of their meal and their enthusiasm has been moderated to an acceptable level.

A seven-year-old child we know came home from a friend's house with some rather fantastic stories his friend had told him, and he told them to his parents with total conviction. He truly believed the things he had been told, and when he found out a couple of days later that they were simply the fabrications of a creative mind, he was upset and declared that he couldn't trust his friend anymore. This sort of thing continued to happen and went so far as to involve a tale of the friend being followed and approached by a strange man. Up to this point they had just been childish stories, but now, where safety was an issue, our friend decided to speak with the friend's parent. The friend's parent sighed and said that their child had a fertile imagination and didn't always know where to separate fact from fiction.

After another incident supposedly involving a call to the police because someone was trying to break in their back door (as told to the seven-year-old), our friend called the parent to ask if the perpetrator had been apprehended. The parent said no such thing had happened and promised to speak to the child about being truthful, but essentially dismissed it as a childish fancy. Our friend's child learned that he could not believe everything he heard, that he cannot always trust even friends to tell him the truth. Lying is lying, whether it involves the inconsequential or the serious.

Silliness and pointless chatter have also been issues—divided as to gender, at least in our house. Jennifer has always been the high-speed chatterbox and gets so carried away with the sound of her own voice that she forgets about her schoolwork or chores and even other people's desires to say a word or two.

"Hush, child," we sometimes have to say. "You're speaking so quickly we can't understand you." And then when she does slow down below the sound barrier, we sometimes have to point out that she's not saying anything of earthshaking importance. "Take a minute and decide what it is you *really* want to tell us." We don't want to discourage her desire to communicate with us, but we do want to help her get to the point and share the air time with others.

Andrew, on the other hand, is more rowdy and silly than chatty. One day he tumbled through the kitchen and bounced off a wall or two, acting like the fourth Stooge and sounding like a full barrel of deranged howler monkeys. Dan looked at Elizabeth and remarked, "Somewhere, a village is missing its idiot." The phrase stuck, and we worked it into a routine for notifying Andrew when his behavior was inappropriate.

We admire Andrew for his offbeat sense of humor and his weird and wacky ways, but not at the dinner table or at other times when unrestrained levity isn't appreciated. That's when we say, "You're welcome to join us for a meal, Andrew, but the village idiot is not. So come and sit down peacefully and leave the idiot elsewhere until we're finished."

What we model will show up at our dinner table. Jennifer likes to repeat what she hears her friends say. Sometimes she might be testing the validity of the information, to see what Mom and Dad have to say on the subject. As long as it's not gossip or silly chattering, we acknowledge her contributions to our conversation and place our stamp of approval on her willingness to include us in her life. But we don't need—or want—to hear everything. Generally, they may tell us what they have seen or heard themselves, but we discourage them from repeating stories told by a third party.

We try to help them define what is and is not our business. The family dinner table is a place for candid discussion, but it is hard to encourage openness and equip our children to be involved in society without getting into discussions of other people's doings or weaknesses. Such talk could be destructive gossip if it went beyond our inner circle of four. At these times we have explicitly defined the limits of the conversation, pointing out that some things we discuss among ourselves would be hurtful if repeated to anyone else. The children have respected this confidence, and within this sphere of privacy we have helped them to respond properly to such pressing problems as having a friend who habitually lies to them or relatives who don't keep their well-intentioned promises.

What's true for them as children is true for us as adults: when our tongues are under control, communication is a mutual pleasure.

—12—

Drugs & Beyond

Moderation & Self-Control

Children must understand both the therapeutic and recreational qualities of drugs and alcohol and learn to distinguish use from abuse.

The more we as parents have talked about the appeal and dangers of drugs and alcohol, the more we have wondered what we are teaching our kids about medicine at home.

When we say, "Take this pill, drink this syrup, it will make you feel better," aren't we simply laying the ground for the children deciding that drugs are there specifically to make them *feel* better instead of *making* them better?

Medicine is there to help make our bodies *healthy;* such things as taste and feeling better are secondary issues. (Anyone who has endured aggressive chemotherapy will agree that the cure is almost as bad as the disease.) True, we will eventually feel better when we are healthy, as medicine is intended to help our bodies be strong, to function properly and in balance.

There is also a use for painkilling medicines, but when we fail to make these clear we are setting the stage for *any* pharmaceutical product to be used primarily as a feel-better painkiller. And make no mistake about it, that's why recreational drugs are consumed: to feel better by killing the pain inside.

Painkillers are suitable for the temporary elimination or reduction of severe physical pain from illness or injuries, or for numbing unyielding agony in the terminally ill. But painkillers are *not* appropriate for the relief of heartache, loneliness, fear, anxiety or boredom. Addiction is never a healthy thing, but it frequently results when we seek the wrong cure for a problem that won't go away.

In some ways we've had little direct educating to do in this area with our children. We ourselves don't smoke and have only a few relatives who do. The same applies to drinking; we two adults have a glass of wine once or twice a year in celebration of special things, but alcohol is not an important part of our lives. The children are aware that in other societies and other lands wine is an unremarked part of daily life, even for believers. We have explained that *drunkenness* is the problem, not drinking itself, and that Christianity and the moderate intake of alcohol are not incompatible. However, in our society which seems to find moderation both a difficulty and a burden, perhaps it is wiser never to start than to have trouble finding the proper boundaries.

Part of our children's exposure has been common sense rather than "moral." Both children have seen the wrecked cars in the junkyard and watched the "film-at-six" of lives shattered by alcohol and drugs. They have recoiled at the smell of cigarettes in public places and helped us clean the disgusting yellow stains from the walls of our rental house.

Yet some of their friends in later years will smoke and drink; they may marry into families where such habits have long been practiced. We've tried to lay a foundation by explaining the nature of addiction—that some habits, once established, are viciously difficult to break, even with the help of friends, doctors and medication, and even if the person hates doing it and knows it to be unhealthy, destructive and expensive. We have tried to separate our disgust at the habits from our compassion for the people who are stuck with them.

But these examples may be too easy, as life can be lived without alcohol and tobacco. Food is a different issue; we may become addicted to food (or certain kinds of food), yet we can't stay away from eating altogether. Avoidance becomes an issue of self-control, consuming only what is necessary and appropriate without indulging our appetites. Elizabeth struggles with this because in her teens, food was her security and gratification.

It's acceptable in most Christian circles to be overweight but not to be alcoholic, yet the Bible has more references to gluttony than to drunkenness. Why do we heed one warning and not the other? Do our eating habits tell our children that the comfort and abuse of food is acceptable but not drugs or alcohol? What, ultimately, is the difference? The only earthly distinctions may be societal and legal; the police will not arrest you for eating french fries while driving, and chocolate breath is not socially offensive. In spiritual terms, any abuse is damaging to our "temple."

For very young children, example can be sufficient. Elizabeth was raised in a home where carbonated beverages were restricted and Coke was never permitted; however, she was never told *why.* She grew up with the idea that Coke was like alcohol and cigarettes—something that was bad for you, did not please God and could compromise a person's Christian witness.

One day when she was about eight, she was with a group of Christians who were sharing the gospel in a public place. One of the young men disappeared for a few minutes and then returned sipping a bottle of Coke. Elizabeth was shocked that he would drink the vile stuff while witnessing to the unsaved!

It was several years later, well after she had come to realize that Coke was simply a sugar-laden, caffeinated beverage, that she shared this with her parents. They laughed, and her mother explained that the reason she had never allowed Coke in the house was that she had seen it spilled on the rubber tiles of her school when she was a child and couldn't help but notice the permanent damage it had done to the floor. "If that's what it did to rubber tiles, imagine what it could do to the inside of my children's stomachs!"

To this day Elizabeth does not care for Coke and does not allow the children to drink it. However, she has learned to reluctantly tolerate her husband's taste for it.

The example we set for the children will go far for them, but it is not enough. As the children grow, they need to know *why*. For some children that may not be enough. Some seem set on challenging every standard their parents set for them. Some have to learn the hard way.

One night we watched *The Seven Per Cent Solution* with Andrew—a video we might not have let him see had Dan remembered the brief but bloody shooting at the end. But there was a good, unplanned side to our error; the movie portrayed Sherlock Holmes's recovery from cocaine addiction and depicted the hallucinatory horrors of withdrawal through his eyes. Andrew was both fascinated and repelled by the weird distortions and dreams of beasts and snakes, and asked several questions that led us into a great discussion of drugs, drug effects and drug addiction. We couldn't have planned a better insight into the long-term perils of recreational drugs; our plans would probably have included an overcooked lecture and a verbal description of nervous system overload that would have made no sense to him. This way, by human accident (but probably divine intervention), we could say a few words and let the movie do the rest.

By the time our children do enter college and the workplace, they will already have made up their minds on these issues, and it will take major events to change those attitudes. Toward that end, we've tried to lay out for them a set of practical questions that could be asked about any activity or product, not just the obvious subjects of alcohol, tobacco and illegal drugs:

☐ Will it actually make your life better or just deaden the pain?

☐ Are the immediate costs acceptable?

☐ Will there be unacceptable costs later on, long after the pleasure or benefit is gone?

The greatest gift we can give them here is to make their current reality one they won't need to escape from; if they have an interesting and satisfying life that needs no added "pleasures" and has no chronic pain to deaden, they will have fewer problems saying no.

—13—

Horror &
the Occult

*"It is necessary to have an orthodox and
circumspect belief in the supernatural in order
to avoid being taken in by bogus versions."*
Thomas E. Porter

Not all the real world is visible, and not all that is unseen is safe. Children must be shown the difference and led toward the shelter of the only true knowledge and power. We wrote this section in the depths of October, surrounded by the trappings of Halloween—a holiday that seems to grow bigger and more sinister every year. Figures of ghosts, goblins and ghouls adorn all the stores, whether they're actually selling Halloween items or not. Witches and witchcraft are "hot," whether in the new TV sitcoms or the latest books for "young adults." A weekly paper is published here for students of New Age philosophies and witchcraft; witches advertise openly, speaking high praises of their powers and spreading the influence of their covens. Our daily paper (which has a Scripture verse on the front page) also prints astrological predictions, and Toys "R" Us sells Ouija boards.

How have we handled all this?

We have made it no secret that the spiritual world is real but unseen.

We don't explain away *all* scary things as "figments of the imagination."

Rather, we explain the nature of both sides of God's spiritual creation and point to the protection offered to us by allegiance and obedience to God and his serving spirits, the angels.

We don't have much choice, for Christianity *is* supernatural—in all of the shades of meaning of that word:

☐ It is not a human-made or humanly discovered faith/religion; it was given to us as God's act of self-revelation.

☐ It deals with such intangible and non-"natural" things as the Holy Spirit, our spirit, angelic spirits and demonic spirits. It speaks openly and frankly of spiritual warfare, of unseen armies and invisible enemies, and "war in the heavenlies."

Occult means "hidden," and much of the appeal is tied to the curiosity factor. There is something in all of us that thrills at the prospect of gaining access to "forbidden knowledge"—secrets too deep and powerful to be shared with ordinary people. That power is the other half of the dark equation. Who wouldn't like to have dark forces at their command, with a store of spells ready for difficult situations and personal pleasure?

Curiosity and power . . . a potentially irresistible combination for anyone who doesn't know (or recognize) the power of God and the truth which, when known, sets us free. *If we don't talk to our children about evil spirits and dark powers, they will find someone who will.*

And the appeal of the occult is true, to a point. The "hidden" part was hidden for a reason, and the power is real—but deceptive, limited, temporary, evil and of Satan himself.

We have a better option—one that introduces us to power in the form of a loving, incarnate Person. Christianity is the opposite of the occult in many ways:

☐ Christianity is an "open secret," available to anyone who wants to understand.

☐ Christianity is an "open society," open to anyone who *will* come.

☐ Christianity is the light against the darkness, but it is not an equal battle. Darkness does not destroy light; it is light that destroys the darkness. (Stated another way, light is not the absence of darkness; darkness is the absence of light.) Ephesians 6:12 gives us the biblical perspective: "For our struggle is not against flesh and blood, but against the rulers, against the authorities, against the powers of this dark world and against the spiritual forces of evil in the heavenly realms."

Our family was going through some rocky times created by external pressures. One night Jennifer woke up about midnight, very upset, saying there was a presence of evil in her room and she was afraid to sleep there. We let her sleep on the floor in our room. The next night she was in tears at bedtime, with the same explanation.

We listened to her try to explain it, but since it was getting well past her bedtime, again allowed her to sleep in our room. This went on for several nights, with us praying with her and lying beside her as she was trying to go to sleep. We sat in her room, open to experiencing whatever was going on. Was this merely an overactive imagination? Perhaps, but we treated it as the real thing, partly because we did feel that our family was under some sort of spiritual attack and didn't want to take any chances if it was the real thing, and partly because we wanted Jennifer to know that we believed her and respected her feelings.

We called several friends who knew of our present circumstances and declared a prayer war. Things settled down within a few days.

Were our daughter's fears based on something satanic that was pressing in around us? Possibly. To dismiss them as childish fears would only have encouraged her to be afraid when she didn't have to, and allowed her imagination to entertain ideas of the "spirit world" as it affected her. The only spirit we want affecting our children is the Holy Spirit, the Spirit of the Lord, the God of this universe!

As part of our stand we have chosen not to celebrate Halloween as others do. We are reluctant to forbid our children to participate in the neighborhood activities because we remember the great fun we had as children. But that was thirty or more years ago, and what innocence was there is fading fast. Halloween has become an international festival that everyone can celebrate—Christmas and Easter are too Christian for many (unless the religious symbols can be removed), while Hanukkah and Passover are Jewish. But Halloween is universal because everyone believes in (or is willing to pretend to believe in) ghosts, goblins, witches and vampires for a night.

Halloween is also a big-bucks retail event, but that's not our main difficulty. Halloween draws attention to and glorifies the realm of evil—Satan and his evil spirits. Halloween tries to make it all cute and adorable and fun, but that's not the reality. We don't want our children, our home, or any of our resources used to promote a celebration that points to Satan.

We have tried to find a *different* way and reason to celebrate. In the past we have used Halloween for a special family game and treat night; we turn off our porch light, which in this area lets the trick-or-treaters know to skip our house. (We have also shared the family time with another family.) We do prefer the autumn celebrations and decorations to reflect "harvest" themes, which, after all, is a most important event here in the heart of Indiana. Some churches have "Saints' Parties" on All Saints' Day (November 1); our church once had a "Hallelujah" party with appropriate costumes, games, activities and treats in the form of a praise and worship time.

Recently, however, we were confronted with a new dilemma. Our children's piano teacher arranged for her music studio students to present a recital (in costume) at our neighborhood Halloween festival. After some discussion we eventually agreed to let our children wear a costume to play their piano pieces and to participate in the costume contest and parade.

We had reservations. Are the costumes wrong in themselves? As a fantasy enthusiast (both reader and writer) Dan says no, there is nothing inherently wrong with pretending to be something we're not. Children do it all the time, with our approval, when they play doctor or nurse or fireman or race-car driver. Our children often dressed up to imitate their heroes, whether imaginary, famous or closer to home; Jennifer tried on Elizabeth's shoes, or Andrew wore Dan's short summer robe around the house.

It's one natural way to practice for the future. But what are we pretending to be? Something we would be if we could? Or something we really shouldn't be? We did have a problem with the idea of *disguises* as opposed to *costumes.* Whatever we grow up to be, or want to become, the personal part of "us" should still be recognizable in the end product. And the rules we finally laid down for our children reflected our understanding:

1. They could participate in the costume contest and parade if they wished, though we did not encourage it.

2. The costumes had to be of a worthy hero or heroine, whether current, historical or fictional.

3. Their faces couldn't be covered with a mask or made up beyond easy recognition.

We attended the festival as a family and had a great deal of fun. The children both won prizes for their costumes, created in accordance with our rules. Jennifer was Princess Leia; though a member of a civilization that misunderstands the nature of God, she is at least a virtuous and exciting heroine. Andrew was a World War 2 bomber pilot, in his leather and wool jacket, black snow boots, aviator glasses and old-fashioned headphones; as members of our family have served in civil occupations aligned with the armed forces, we enjoyed his tribute.

The calls aren't always that clear. This year Andrew planned to go with his good friend as *Men [Boys?] in Black.* We agreed, after due discussion, because the movie did leave room for God as the creator of alien nations and did support the maintenance of inter-galactic justice. Yet we discouraged Jennifer from her original plan of dressing up as a Gypsy girl. There was simply too much identi-fication in our minds with the lawless supernatural, with fortune-telling and dark spiritual secrets. We were able to extend the discussion to contrast Ouija boards and astrological predictions with the guidance of Scripture, and talk about King Saul's devas-tatingly successful attempt to raise the dead (1 Samuel 28).

Whatever our strategy, defending against evil requires an accu-rate and personal theology of evil (which is itself personal) and a reliance on the true spiritual power, the Lord and Creator of the universe. In order to avoid the counterfeit we must help our children seek and recognize the genuine.

—14—

Sex &
Sexuality

*A child is a sexual creature and
has a sexual identity and vulnerability long
before developing an interest in sex.
Children have to be shown the beautiful part of
their sexuality and the necessity of
guarding it from the world.*

No doubt about it, each one of our children is not only
different, but of a different sex. We noticed this right away,
but the kids took a few years to catch on.

As a three-year old, Jennifer watched and tried to help with
changing Andrew's diapers. One day she asked what *that* was on
him.

Elizabeth explained that it was his penis. "Boys, like Andrew,
have a penis, and girls, like you, have a vulva," she told her. That
was all she wanted (and needed) to know at that point.

As Andrew grew and was being potty-trained, Jennifer noticed
that he could stand up to urinate. That fascinated her for as long
as it took her to try standing too. She lost interest quickly.

When they graduated from diapers, we instructed them in the
"good touch/bad touch" knowledge, reminding them that *no one* had
a right to touch their private parts without their permission. If it

was a medical necessity, a doctor or nurse could examine them, but only in a clinic or emergency room or on the scene of an accident. Even then, we the parents would probably be present as well.

For a while the children took baths together. It was a wonderful playtime for them as brother and sister. They both felt very comfortable being naked in front of each other, but when Jennifer was eight or so, she began to talk about her "privacy." She shrieked if Andrew saw her in her underwear, but occasionally she still wanted to take a bath with him so they could play with their neat tub toys. We decided to let Jennifer choose when she no longer wanted to share bathtime. We felt that if we imposed a rule about it, she might feel a sense of shame that we didn't want her to experience. We've been pleased to see it happen gradually and very naturally.

When they were *very* young, we tried to neither flaunt nor hide our own nakedness as parents. When the children were toddlers, they trotted around when Elizabeth lay back in the tub or dashed back to the bedroom to get dressed. They would "visit" Dan in the shower, peeking around the curtain to see what all the splashing was about. They would walk in on us while we were dressing, and we didn't scramble to cover ourselves.

We gradually restricted such accidental exposure as they grew, partially along gender lines. We wanted both Jennifer and Andrew to have some sense of what they would look like as adults; we hoped the changes that would come upon them would be less frightening if they knew that we had passed that way before them.

Yet we tried to teach them modesty and privacy as well. They observed that we didn't go outside in next-to-nothing and that there were appropriate times for walking around upstairs in our underwear. Now, of course, we close our bedroom door while dressing and instruct them to knock and wait for permission before entering. The children themselves have decided when to close their bedroom doors while dressing and in what stages of undress they will allow themselves to be seen.

More Than Simple Biology

When we parents were young, traditional sex education began and ended with the standard (gender-segregated) school lecture-and-film-and-book illuminating the biology and mechanics of sex, meaning intercourse and the process of birth. But that is only a small part of what we must pass on to our children, for further dangers and problems have arisen, and their sexuality is truly so much more than the mere functions of the body.

A certain level of education about sexuality is present every day as we live out our marriage. The children witness our affectionate pats and our intermittent spats. They know that our bedroom is special; it is ours to share with each other and not with them unless they are specifically invited in for a talk or a snuggle.

They observe how we celebrate our wedding anniversaries and Valentine's Day. They see us kiss (more than just a passing peck on the cheek). They know we disappear on occasional dates, both in and out of the house. They see us hold hands. When we all watch TV together, they are reminded again that Mom and Dad sit together—kids sit on the outside, not in the middle. Except on special occasions or when sibling relief is needed on long trips Mom and Dad ride in the front seat of the van so they can hold hands and talk easily, and the kids get the back seat. They have been explicitly informed that we were married to each other long before they showed up, and we intend to still be married long after they have grown up, moved out and established homes of their own.

They learn a few things from watching us.

We enjoy each other. There are lots of hugs and pats and back-scratches and terms of affection freely shared between the two of us. Intimate companionship is neither dirty nor evil; it is God's plan for one man and one woman who have restricted their activities to one permanent relationship.

We make time for each other as a priority which often temporarily eclipses the children. Elizabeth may take a few minutes to curl up in Dan's arms on the couch sometime during the evening. If asked a question by one of the kids, her answer may be "We're busy. If it doesn't involve fire, blood or broken bones, you can come back later." If mealtime is approaching, the meal planned is casual and we are aware that the kids are interested in an acceptable TV special or video, we may give them license to eat in front of the TV while we two adults rendezvous at the Café Al Fresco on the back porch to share our own meal.

We can disagree and express different opinions without damaging our relationship. We are compatible, but not identical or interchangeable, and we show the results of our different upbringings. We can discuss, analyze and argue without fighting—right out in front of the children—with humor and acceptance, and without raising fears of animosity and divorce.

The resultant message is both explicit and implicit: "We love you very much, but we've loved each other longer, and we need to be husband and wife even more than we need to be your parents."

"But Why?"

Setting a good example for them is a great start, but it's not enough. We were raised simply with "thou shalt not." However, it really does help to understand the *why.* Sex outside of marriage is dangerous: unwanted pregnancy, sexually transmitted diseases (STDs), physical commitment that usually leads to emotional commitment without the security of a lifelong covenant. God reserved the sexual expression of love for the marriage relationship. He established this for our benefit, and he has our best interest in mind. His laws and principles are to protect us, not to stop us from having fun. (Actually this concept must be passed on to the children for *all* areas of God's law, not only in sexual matters.)

Our children have seen some of the results of defying those principles.

Elizabeth works with the local Crisis Pregnancy Center, a volunteer organization that helps women deal with unexpected or difficult pregnancies. The staff shares medical and spiritual truths with the clients, giving them accurate information about abortion, adoption and parenting in the hope that they will choose life for their unborn child. Elizabeth frequently takes the "hot line" so that twenty-four-hour service is maintained. This means that the phone may ring in the middle of supper, the middle of a bedtime story or the middle of the night. Our children can often hear Elizabeth's side of the conversation and gain some sense of the frustration, fear and pain that the callers are bearing.

When Jennifer and Andrew were seven and three respectively, a pregnant fourteen-year-old girl came to live with us for the last seven months of her term. It was an adjustment and education for everybody. Elizabeth wrote these notes about that time in our lives:

Tanya was the second daughter in her family. She was quiet and, except for when she was alone with me, was essentially uncommunicative. At family meals she wouldn't participate in the conversation unless specifically asked a question or the subject revolved around her and her interests.

Tanya agreed to go through some workbooks with me, to help her prepare to be a mother. She was choosing to raise her child herself. These sessions led to a few interesting discussions, and although the gospel was clearly presented, Tanya showed no interest in her spiritual condition. She willingly attended church and church functions with us.

Tanya was faithful in carrying out her household chores, and except for having to ask her to say please, thank you and excuse me, and to refrain from using God's name inappropriately, we never had to correct her.

We don't specifically know if the experience made any difference to Tanya, but we don't see how it could not have left at least some deep impressions in her young heart and mind. In our home she was welcomed as a part of the family but free to come and go as she needed to with her real family. In our home she was not yelled at or exposed to filthy language or violent behavior. In our home she was not permitted to watch just any television program she desired; there were restrictions. In our home there was a gentle and very present father figure. Although she never commented on it, she must have observed the love and respect with which we treated one another.

But we do know what differences it made to us. We learned a lot, very quickly, about a whole side of life we'd never participated in. The value system carried in Tanya's mind was so foreign from mine. I found myself struggling to connect with her. It was difficult to identify with her and her ideas about parenting and life in general, but after several sessions alone with her, one day it hit me. Tanya and I weren't so different from each other after all. In fact, we were very much alike. We were each following in the footsteps of our own mothers, making similar life choices, and living out our lives as our mothers had modeled theirs. We just had very different models!

We planted seeds. We hope that someday someone will be able to see the fruit. It was hard to let go and feel that there was no visible change in Tanya for having been with us. Our daughter remembers the girl who, just a year and a half older than she is now, sat in our kitchen, heavy with child, and said that she was going to be a good mother to her baby.

The last time we saw her, Tanya had three children. They were thin, with dull, vacant looks in their wide eyes. They looked just like their mother.

Jennifer, at least, is old enough to understand all this. She began volunteering at the nearby Crisis Pregnancy Center office when she was 11, folding clothes and doing odd chores, but still seeing all the heartbreak that the clients carry in with them. She joins the staff in their prayers and is getting exactly what we hoped for: exposure to the ways and woes of the world without having to make the mistakes herself.

—15—

Entertainment

*Toys, television, books, magazines, radio, music,
movies, videos and computers will all
strive to fill up our children's minds with their
often-destructive content.
We can help them learn to analyze their
entertainment, discern the messages presented
and turn away from the unworthy.*

I n the beginning, children *are entertainment, but it's not long*
before they *need* entertainment. And later, they learn to entertain themselves.

We start with toys, but there are a bewildering variety of them
to choose from. How do we pick the good ones?

We embraced the toys that were well-made, simple and encouraged building, fitting and manipulating the pieces. Blocks, simple
puzzles and Duplo were ideal. (We stayed away from toys that were
battery-powered, partly because we didn't want to keep buying
batteries, but mostly because we wanted our kids to provide the
motive power.)

We stayed away from toys with questionable powers or occult
connections—He-Men, Transformers, Masters of the Universe—
and other toys which featured ram's heads, pyramids or astrological symbols.

We tried to steer our children away from toys which set up unrealistic expectations—like Barbie.

We tried to avoid toys which were linked to cartoons, for cartoons (among other things) establish the way the toy should act and behave rather than freeing the children to act out their own stories with the figures. (Jennifer delighted in the *My Little Pony* figures, but was basically uninterested in the TV show. Her imagination was richer and far more compelling than the Hollywood writers.) We evaluated which came first, the interest in the toy as a toy (perhaps from seeing it in the store or at a friend's house) or the interest provoked by the TV show?

The Tyranny of the TV

We didn't let our kids watch commercial cartoons *(Bugs Bunny, Roadrunner, Tom and Jerry)* until we felt they could distinguish fantasy-comic violence from real violence.

To the very young child a cartoon is a documentary.

(Andrew at 18 months) *Tonight you decided to walk on your hands and feet, then every so often fall flat on the floor on your tummy, and laugh and laugh. I wondered what you were doing, where you had gotten this idea, since I'd never seen Jennifer doing anything like this. Then it hit me! We just bought the video "Bambi," and you've been watching Bambi lose his footing on the ice and fall on his tummy. You get down on all fours and do likewise. You're a smart little critter. You watch things carefully and do your best to "go and do likewise." We have to keep a close watch on you.*

When they were young, we allowed them a diet of videos and selected public TV shows:

Ages 2-6

☐ *Shining Time Station* (and *Thomas the Tank Engine* videos)

☐ *Winnie the Pooh*

☐ selected Disney videos and movies

☐ *Mr. Rogers' Neighborhood*

☐ *Sesame Street*

☐ *Reading Rainbow*
Ages 7-12
☐ *Bill Nye the Science Guy*
☐ local zoo show
☐ *3-2-1 Contact*
☐ *Wishbone*
(We don't have cable, though that may change if our local cable companies will ever let us pick and choose which channel ones we want instead of the one-exorbitant-price-buys-everything package.)

When they were seven or eight, we began to let them watch selected Saturday morning cartoons, with strict guidelines and clear discussions.

"You know this is all make-believe," we said. "A real animal or person would die if you dropped an anvil on his head. He wouldn't get up again, shake away the stars around his head and start the chase again."

Andrew has enjoyed the *Three Stooges* this last year, but we were careful not to publicize their existence until he was old enough to identify and appreciate pretend violence.

What can they watch now?
☐ news
☐ sports (with Dad, generally)
☐ any shows they watched as younger kids, if they're still interested
☐ rented movies (with parental approval)

The video store near us has frequent 47-cent specials, and the public library has an interesting collection of older films. When Andrew expressed an interest in seeing the original *Frankenstein* and *Wolfman* movies, Dan watched them with him, and they spent quite a bit of time discussing the issues involved. Do werewolves and other evil monsters exist? What was the problem with Dr. Frankenstein's monster? Was it right for the scientist to play God? (Nearly any incident can become the springboard for good discussion and a "learning moment" *if* the precedent has been established *and* the situation is handled properly.)

We adults recently rented and previewed two videos with the same PG-13 rating. *The Tuskegee Airmen,* the story of black American fighter pilots in World War II, contained rough language, racial hatred, blood and sudden death, yet we felt it was very appropriate for both kids to see with us. It was sad, shocking, triumphant and historical. It told our kids something they needed to know about the history of our country. Andrew watched it several times, was able to link it with a visit to a Tuskegee Airmen display at our local museum and eventually acquired the G.I. Joe Tuskegee Airman figure.

The other film, *Lightning Jack,* contained profanity and crude sexual jokes and could not be redeemed by the many funny moments. We did not allow the kids to watch the man they know from other acceptable films indulging in bathroom humor and instructing a younger man in the sexist mechanics of coupling with a saloon girl.

We're constantly reminded that the ratings process is not consistent and isn't based on *our* set of values. Sex, violence and language aren't the only objectionable content possible. After a few viewings, we eliminated *The Ugly Dachshund* from our family viewing because of the way in which the father was portrayed—a well-intentioned but bumbling guy who was easily manipulated by the mother and the kids. Otherwise, it was funny and clean but not the kind of viewpoint we wanted to encourage.

Screening videos takes time and isn't always convenient, but there are some side benefits. We have had some cheap dates together and have been better prepared for joint discussions with the kids. (If a film is G, we will now consider letting them watch it unscreened. Their filters have been pretty well tuned by now, and they know what is appropriate behavior for them—whether or not Hollywood agrees with us!)

The home environment has an impact as well. Andrew could not have handled the big-screen, unrelenting tension of *The Lost World* in the theater, but he was able to watch it on our 13-inch TV in video form. The surroundings were familiar, the sound and image weren't overwhelming, and we could stop the tape to take a break or talk about what was happening.

We allow them to watch *Touched by an Angel;* though not a profoundly Christian show, it handles controversial and painful issues from a highly moral and mostly Biblical framework. They can learn about these things from an outside perspective, from within the safety of their own homes. The same usually applies to *COPS* and *Real TV,* though Mom and Dad generally control the remote and have to be ready to make explanations.

We want our children to enjoy and appreciate TV, but not be addicted to it. We have to give them alternatives, and not neglect them personally, or *send* them to watch TV as a method of getting them out of our hair. The appeal of TV has been somewhat dimmed by the emphasis in our house on reading. This is a house full of books, and the children have learned that printed words plus their own imagination are often more powerful than stories spelled out for them on film. (A picture may be worth a thousand words, but sometimes the thousand words are more interesting.)

Radio and Music

Dan was a disc jockey for a small radio station the early 1970s, and Elizabeth has trained in classical piano. There is music in our house, but it is not limited to any single variety. Dan has a taste for selected rock, blues and bluegrass, while Elizabeth prefers piano and classical music.

Our approach to music is little different than our approach to other forms of media. We have discussed the meaning of many songs we play or hear on the radio, because understanding the lyrics and message of popular music gives us a bridge to our culture. (Dan, in particular, feels that the lyrics of much modern music are more honest than those of some Christian songs.)

It is not unusual to hear one of our children say, "I like that music. What's the song about?" That's when we turn to the lyrics, sometimes they're on the album (remember those?) or CD sleeve, and sometimes we have to find them at the library or on the Internet. We can also research the artist's public/private life and discuss how it affects their lyrics and music.

Dan sat in a pizza place with some teenagers not long ago and listened to the jukebox. One girl was humming along to the music.

"What's that song about?" he asked her. "I'm having a hard time following the lyrics."

"I don't know," she answered. "I just like it for the music."

Further discussion revealed that she owned the CD. Therefore, some of her money had gone to enrich the artist, the record company and the retailer for this music she knew so little about. What message was her money sending? *Let's have more of the same . . . whatever that is.*

Gambling

When Dan was young, his father taught him and his sister in one easy lesson, *how* to gamble and why *not* to gamble. He divided a stack of Monopoly money equally among them, explained the basic rules of poker and then cleaned them out. Then he gave them back their money, showed them how to play dice and cleaned them out again.

The lesson was clear: Do this for fun if you want to, but not for money.

Elizabeth, on the other hand, grew up in a church environment where face cards were forbidden, although games like *Authors* and *Old Maid* were permitted. When we play cards with our friends now, *Euchre, Hearts* or *Spades,* she occasionally has to think about the difference between spades and clubs.

We started playing *Go Fish* and *Old Maid* with our children and have graduated to a simplified version of *Spades.* We've used these occasions to try to make clear the distinction between skill and chance: chance dictates the cards they are dealt, but skill determines how well they do with the cards they have. (There is a larger life lesson in that as well; someday it may sink in.)

Computer and the Internet

Should children be allowed free access to every book, magazine and video in every bookstore, entertainment mall and video shop?

Of course not.

Yet many parents seem to think it appropriate to give their children full and unrestricted access to the Internet.

Unfortunately, most schools and public libraries are on the side of the *public* and not on the side of the *parent*. Our public libraries here, at least, are afraid to restrict any patron's access lest they be accused of censorship. Parents *can* have their children's library cards marked to limit the ratings of videos they can borrow, but no such limitations apply to Internet access through the library's computers.

Yet the very nature of the Internet *is* unrestricted access.

There are electronic safeguards (SafeSurf, NetNanny, Cyber Patrol), but they don't always work. (In many cases, the kids know more about computers than their parents and teachers combined.)

And pornography isn't the only problem on the Internet. Every group (and individual) with an agenda and the technology has a website, and the features range from Nazi hate propaganda and witchcraft to bomb-building.

For this stage of their lives we have chosen to *monitor* access, rather than *restrict* it. Due to Dan's talents with rebuilding discarded equipment, there are several computers around the house. But only two have modems, and only one has full Internet access. That one is Dan's laptop, and he takes the kids on-line with him when there is a need.

Jennifer does have her own America Online e-mail address in order to send e-mail to her friends and her "wired" aunt, but Dan was careful to select a user name for her that doesn't betray her gender, her real name or her age. In addition, he used the built-in options to select an appropriate level of access for her.

Our children have passed from the "blinder" stage to the point where their "filters" are operational if not yet fully developed; we will continue with our loving and shaping, working toward the hope of Philippians 1:9-11:

> And this is my prayer: that your love may abound more and more in knowledge and depth of insight, so that you may be able to discern what is best and may be pure and blameless until the day of Christ, filled with the fruit of righteousness that comes through Jesus Christ—to the glory and praise of God.

—16—

Weapons &
Warfare

Little boys (in particular) are fascinated with
guns, explosions, machines and noise
—everything, in fact, that makes up war and
drives warriors. The problem is
how to teach the necessity and worth of
occasional armed conflict
without glorifying it. We can be
"people of peace" while acknowledging that
we "do not bear a sword in vain."

We *initially told our relatives, "No toy guns for the kids."*
We've had to change the rules a few times since then. The
first occasion arose when a visiting six-year-old showed
our three-year-old Jennifer how to build a gun out of her Duplo.
She was delighted to learn something new to do with her blocks,
though she didn't care that it was a gun.

When Andrew came along, he discovered that he didn't need a
toy weapon—he already had a gun on the end of each arm. (The
ultimate point-and-shoot offense!) As a corollary to this discovery,
he also realized that he could create a gun out of toy bricks, Lincoln
Logs or any appropriately bent stick. We quickly realized that our
children were going to be exposed to toy guns at the homes of
friends as well, so we decided to allow some toy weapons under

some newly established ground rules.

It Isn't Polite to Point

Rule 1: Don't point any weapon (pretend or real) at anything alive. (That includes, specifically, any parent or sibling and the house cats; generally included are the squirrels that climb into the bird feeder and even the flowers in the garden.) Designated targets and inanimate objects (rocks, trees) are okay. (We parents just have to get used to the suction-cup arrow stuck on the refrigerator door.)

The children each had a Super Soaker the summer Andrew was four and Jennifer was seven. They could blast away at each other, but only when we said they could, and only when both parties agreed. If they fired without permission, the Super Soaker would be confiscated for two weeks.

One hot afternoon Andrew had his weapon loaded, in his hand, when opportunity knocked. There was his sister on the back deck, cornered, without her Super Soaker. We saw his brain click into gear; a grin erupted across his face and he fired at will—making his sister shriek and holler—partly from surprise and partly from fun. He emptied the barrel of water all over her and, still grinning, handed us his weapon. He knew the penalty and had chosen to pay it for the moment of delight. The Super Soaker was confiscated for two weeks, but we had to smile as we put it away.

Safety Is the Priority

Rule 2: Real weapons are dangerous and must be used safely. Dan, who worked with an engineer who was a shooting enthusiast, arranged to take the whole family to a target range when Andrew was eight and Jennifer was eleven. Our friend Jon brought along his collection of .22 rifles and a brace of shotguns. He gave a brief but complete safety lecture, and then we all began plinking away at the targets with the .22s.

When we examined the targets, we pointed out to the kids how readily even the .22 bullets had penetrated the plywood backing. "Your skin is a lot softer than wood!" And they were especially impressed when they saw what damage a shotgun did at close range. The adults went on to sample skeet shooting with the bigger shotguns, while the children lugged the clay "birds" and loaded the traps.

It was a successful outing. The kids literally had a blast, but Elizabeth, who had never held a gun in her life, turned out to be a natural markswoman. We had achieved our objectives: We wanted the children to respect guns without being inordinately fearful, and we wanted them to be able to handle a gun safely if the need arose. We also wanted to satisfy their curiosity without crushing their interest; though shooting was still restricted-access territory, it was no longer unknown and mysterious.

Five Good Reasons

We went on to talk about the purpose of weapons, pointing out five valid reasons that came to mind for carrying and using a weapon.

1. The pioneers needed guns to obtain food, though that's not too relevant to our lives today. (In our area 150 years ago, Andrew would probably have been sent out daily with his rifle to bag squirrels and rabbits for the stewpot.)

2. Sport shooting can be fun, but we don't believe in shooting animals for sport. "I could kill an animal that was endangering people or other animals," said Dan, "but why kill something just for fun? Target shooting I can understand."

3. Though we live in a good neighborhood, and Dan's occupation has been a safe one, there are places and jobs in our city that aren't so secure. "Some people carry guns for protection," Dan pointed out, "and some people keep guns in their house to discourage burglars. If I had one of those jobs, I'd probably carry a revolver on my belt. And if we were stuck living in a dangerous neighborhood, there would be a double-barreled pump shotgun hanging on the wall in the hall where we could get to it in a hurry."

4. The police carry weapons because their job involves keeping lawless and dangerous people from hurting others. "And that's okay; that's their job, and they're trained for it. They know when they put on their badge that they may be killed, and that they may have to kill someone."

5. Soldiers carry the biggest arsenal of all. Again, their job is international justice and national defense.

We tried to put all these things in context. "Where weapons are used, people can die. Is that right? Is that good?" Their answers pleased us, for they realized that neither *yes* nor *no* were adequate responses.

War and Warriors

When we watched *Tuskegee Airmen* together, we didn't apologize for the blood and the pain and the hatred and the language and the fiery deaths.

"This is a true story," we said. "War is a regretful necessity, and in war, people die—sometimes justly, sometimes heroically, sometimes senselessly. These pilots were doing a very good thing—a heroic thing. But heroes bleed, and heroes die. If there weren't any risks, then everybody would be a hero, and heroes wouldn't be special.

"Was what they were doing worth it? The bomber crews they were protecting thought so. The people in Europe they were delivering from Hitler thought so, and I think if you could ask the pilots who were killed in combat, they would say it was worth it, even though they died in the doing."

One of Dan's uncles fought his way ashore at D-day, and Elizabeth's father served in Europe; we have included these stories in our oral family history. A film on the Battle of Britain led to a wide-ranging discussion of the reasons behind WW2 and put understanding behind some of the aircraft models Andrew has collected.

Dan has used these times to discuss reasons for and against war, the morality of snipers and special operations (including the SEALs, of whom he is particularly fond). "Violence for its own sake is addictive," he said, "and I don't want you to get too used to it—on TV, in books, or in your play."

Maintaining Sensitivity

Dan occasionally watched the old *A-Team* TV show, but pointed out that it was as highly unrealistic as Saturday morning cartoons. Not so much in the contrived plots, but in the sustained fantasy that no one was ever hurt in the crowd-pleasing violence. Despite the car chases, thundering explosions and thousands of rounds of high-caliber ammunition expended, no one was ever killed or injured. This kind of show was actually giving people a taste of violence but wasn't telling the whole story about the consequences of violence: pain, blood, death, destruction of property. This kind of show has probably done a lot of damage. It has desensitized viewers to violence, acclimating them to something that looked harmless, but has only led to further violence.

Our children will be exposed to the existence, inevitability and utility of violence, but we can help prevent the process of desensitization and keep their hearts soft by our examples.

Our house has always been animal-friendly, and the aid and comfort are extended to critters not normally viewed as pets. At work Dan once found a mouse stuck in a glue trap, one of the crueler (though environmentally friendly) ways to eradicate mice. (These kinds of traps don't break necks or spread poison, but they immobilize the mouse and hold it fast while it starves to death.)

Dan brought the stuck mouse home in his lunchbox, and we spent twenty or thirty minutes peeling and cutting the terrified little varmint free. (To be precise, Dan did the work, the children watched and helped, and Elizabeth stayed on the far side of the kitchen.) We put it in our critter cage (covered aquarium) when there were only a few scraps of sticky paper attached, and the mouse did the rest. In a few hours he had chewed himself totally free and recovered his composure; Elizabeth and the kids set him free the next day in a local park, out of reach of our cats.

The balance is hard to achieve, but worthwhile: a desire for righteousness plus a kind heart. (Proverbs 12:10 reminds us, "A righteous man cares for the needs of his animal.")

We encourage tenderheartedness and compassion toward people as well. Several years ago during a sweltering summer, Dan looked out the window just as the one-man garbage truck pulled up to collect our trash. "I bet he'd like something cold to drink," said Dan. "Andrew, would you take him out a cold soft drink?" Andrew thought it was a splendid idea and surprised the trash collector almost beyond words. The next week, he asked if he could do it again and kept up the ritual until the routes changed in the late fall. He and Dan still send soft drinks out to the city workers who come around to cut trees or patch the street. After a recent snowfall Andrew was watching out the window so he could help neighbors who came out to shovel their walks.

If Andrew can continue to look at those around him, perceive their needs and be moved to help meet them, he will be less likely to perceive them as targets. We think it's paying off already. Although Andrew likes to play with his G.I. Joes and airplane models, he has some appreciation for their humanity and for the difficult, special role a soldier has to play. Recently, he was investigating a CD-ROM full of computer games and showed us a game he'd found that he had decided not to play any further. It was a DOOM-type game, with animated violence, full-color gore and a shoot-whatever-moves mentality.

"That's right," we said. "You understood the point we wanted to make: this is violence without a point." He nodded absently, his mind already on the next, milder game under consideration.

—17—

Death & Dying

*Death is the last enemy, and dying is its last
weapon. Children need to understand the nature
of death and its limitations in order
to deal with loss, grief and the prospects of the
end of their own life on earth.*

Unfortunately, *by the time children discover how much fun*
life is, they also discover that it is fragile—that this mysterious and awful thing called "death" exists and threatens to
destroy that very life.

As adults we often end up avoiding discussion of subjects that
make us uneasy. So it can be with death. The only experience any
of us has is one-sided—none of us has actually experienced death;
we merely observe it in others. Not talking about it *ever* sends a
message to a child that it is indeed something to be feared, that we
are uncomfortable with it, and that they should be too.

Not the Original Plan
We haven't hidden the fact of death from our children, nor have we
tried to teach them that death is natural. Death is typical, normal,

expected and inevitable at this point, but it was not part of God's original plan and is not part of his long-range plan. Death wasn't present in the Garden of Eden until God slew an animal to cover the humans' sin. And eventually it will have no part at all, except, at best, a vague memory.

Having pets in the house and wildlife around the house has helped. We've been forced to talk about life spans for rabbits and robins; our children have buried mice mauled by our cats in spite of the bells jingling on their necks. We have said our final goodbyes to a cat who lost his final fight with disease; we've buried a hand-raised robin that was killed by a neighbor's cat; we've watched chickens hatch and die within the span of a few moments.

And they have been exposed to the death of people, some whom they have known and loved, some whom they never knew at all.

Providing Cardboard Boxes

But how does one explain to a young child what actually happens when someone dies? Jennifer was told at age three that when a person dies it's only their body, their cardboard box, that actually dies. The special parts of who they really are, the parts of them that laugh, make friends, feel love and excitement, will not die because that's their soul. Even a little child can understand that cardboard boxes don't last forever. They may get damp and soft, or torn or worn out from use. When they are no longer able to contain their contents we dispose of them, but we keep the contents because the contents are what is really important, not the actual box.

This explanation was adequate for her at that point, and other concepts sank in over time. As Jennifer grew we were able to explain that when a person who knew Jesus and had asked him to be their Lord and Savior dies, then that part of them goes to be with him forever, and that someday Jesus will give them a new, very special body, just like his.

We wanted the children to understand something about death and dying before they had to deal with it personally. Part of our motivation came from Elizabeth's childhood struggles with the illness and death of her older brother:

I was six when my eight-year-old brother Danny was diagnosed with leukemia. Shortly after the discovery I was taken to a funeral home while my father paid his respects to one of his friends and visited the grieving family. I sat in the foyer with several other children from church whose parents wouldn't take their children inside. Then my father returned and asked me to come with him. I remember staring at him as all the children stared at me—partly out of surprise, and partly out of jealousy that I was allowed inside the hallowed halls of a building where dead people were. I followed my father down the dimly-lit paneled hallway.

Inside there were adults standing around in small groups, talking quietly. It looked like someone's living room, except there were lots of flowers and an open coffin with a dead man in it. My father took me over to the casket and let me look at it carefully. I commented that the man looked like he was sleeping. After being taken to speak to the bereaved family members I was allowed to return to the foyer where all the other children crowded round to ask what it was really like in there. I told them. They seemed almost disappointed, and soon their chatter resumed.

Years later I realized the significance and value of this visit to the funeral home. My parents had wisely arranged for me to see a dead person (whom I had never met) in his coffin before I would have to see my brother in his.

We have taken our children to funeral home visitations since they were babies—sometimes because we were unable to get a sitter, sometimes because it was family and we knew that people would want to see them, sometimes as an intentional part of their education, and sometimes because, in a somber atmosphere, it is a joy to see a fresh young child full of energy and life. (People have thanked us for bringing them, saying it has been a refreshing distraction.)

Visitation does not have to be a long, drawn-out affair, but it shows the child that a body is peaceful in death. The child then knows from first-hand experience that the stories they may hear from the bully down the street about dead bodies is not true. To prevent a child from seeing a dead body in a casket only makes it more mysterious and, therefore, potentially something to be feared. It provides the parent and child with an opportunity to discuss reactions and questions.

It may be inappropriate to take young children to a funeral simply because they have a hard time sitting quietly for long. If your child can sit through a church service, they can probably handle a funeral or a memorial service if they have an adult caring for them who was not too close to the person who has died.

Children need to learn how to conduct themselves in all of life's situations, and they are going to encounter death and its side effects for the rest of their lives. Teaching them how to do it gracefully is a blessing. Teaching them how to smile, shake hands and simply say, "I'm so sorry for your loss," will equip them with a tool that they will have to reach for regularly. And if it's a tool that will also help them reach out to comfort others who are grieving, it will become even more valuable.

(Not having coping skills can be crippling. We know a woman, now middle-aged, who was never taken to funerals or visitations when she was a child. She grew up with a deep-seated fear and as an adult is unable to bring herself to enter a funeral home, even for close friends and family.)

More to Death Than the Funeral—Helping Children Grieve
Again from Elizabeth's writings:

I was nine when Danny died of leukemia—after almost three years of illness, treatment, remission and more illness. I wasn't helped to grieve at the time of his death; because I was a child, no one took notice of the loss that I, too, was experiencing. Being overlooked showed me that my feelings were not important. I needed someone to say that my loss was just as real and just as big to me as was the loss my parents were experiencing. He was their son, but he was also my big brother, my protector and my hero. I did begin showing classic signs of sibling grief, but no one recognized them as I struggled with fears of my own death. Always a good student, I began having difficulty in school, and friendships became more difficult to maintain. The adolescent years were particularly troubled for me as I tried to work through the usual teenage problems. Even years later I still found myself struggling through deep sadness, loneliness and a sense of inadequacy.

Finally, at the age of thirty-two I attended a grief recovery workshop for sibling loss. It was a life-changing experience, as I came to realize that all the things I had struggled with were typical of surviving siblings, and were in fact indications of my emotional health and strength. I just hadn't known it and neither had my parents.

One of the very important things we can do for a child who has lost a loved one is simply to acknowledge verbally that their loss is significant, and that their feelings of sadness are real, appropriate and nothing to be ashamed of.

When a child loses a parent or a sibling, the surviving family members often are so caught up in their own grief and in the necessary arrangements that the children may be overlooked— cared for by loving friends, relatives or a familiar babysitter, but not included in the grieving process. The child needs to be reminded that they are not being emotionally abandoned by the surviving family members, and that they and their feelings of loss are also very important.

Children grieve differently from adults. Adults tend to "be in mourning" for a period of time, and then as time works its healing, the grieving becomes less pronounced and they manage to cope with the absence of their loved one. Children do their grieving in little bits and pieces. They get distracted by play and friends, and enjoy life to its fullest until they encounter something that reminds them of their loss. Then they are sad and want to be comforted, reassured or left alone for a while. It's like a roller coaster ride for a child, while the adult tends to grieve at a more sedate pace. Because children grieve like this, it can take quite a while for them to work through their loss. Sometimes it takes years because as they grow, they come to a fresh understanding of what has changed in their life as a result of this death, and they grieve some more. If children do not begin grieving at the time of a death, they will have to deal with it later in life. It is a process which cannot be avoided or shortened by suppression, but can be made easier by understanding, compassion and the realization that life has a meaning greater than death.

(Jennifer at eight) *We had to say goodbye to Chessie* [Dan's favorite cat and frequent write-through-the-night companion] *last week. He had been quite ill for weeks—gradually failing more and more, and we realized that he was probably getting to the point where he was uncomfortable. You were crying a fair bit, but we realized that this encounter with the death of a loved animal was something that would help to prepare you for the deaths of loved people that you would experience. You are now learning that time is a great healer. We don't miss Chessie quite as much as we did that first awful day. Also, watching him deteriorate helped prepare you to let go of him and to show you that death could come as a blessed relief.*

Overcoming One of Life's Greatest Fears

Beyond grief for the loss of loved ones comes fear—fear of one's own death.

Shortly after her grandfather died, when Jennifer was four, she asked Elizabeth, "Mommy, you really do love me, don't you?"

"Yes I really do, honey," Mom replied.

"And you don't want me to die, do you?"

"No I don't want you to die."

That satisfied her, for a while at least. But the topic came up a year later, when we visited that same grandfather's grave.

(Jennifer at five) *Just before leaving Montreal we visited the cemetery where Grandpa and Uncle Danny are buried. Perhaps it is part of what has triggered your questions and comments about death and dying. You ask me when you are going to die. You've said*

that you know it hurts to die and that you don't want to. You told
me that you don't want to get buried. I reminded you that it's only
your body, your cardboard box, that gets buried. The part of you that
feels, laughs, loves and cries—the valuable part of who you are—
your soul—doesn't get buried. You'll go to live with Jesus and see
Grandpa since you love Jesus and have him living in your heart.

Dying was not part of God's original plan for his people. It isn't
supposed to be comfortable. It's a terrible consequence of our desire
to follow our own ways instead of God's. We're not trying to help
our children become comfortable with death. We're trying to help
them understand what it is, why it is and how we are to respond when
beloved people, special pets and even unknown masses of people and
entire species of creatures are eradicated from this earth, either by
sudden accident, terrible drawn-out disease, natural disasters or the
wicked scheming in another person's twisted heart.

We have told our children that *being* dead doesn't hurt. What
may happen between being alive and being dead may hurt, but
that's one reason God has given us doctors and medicines and
people who love us very much.

In confronting the fear of death in our children we are confronting
it in ourselves as well. It is a fear that every human must face
somewhere along the way. When they are little we can show our
children that together we can talk about our fears. We grow and learn
together, and someday one of us will be the first to die. As we have
learned together, we hope that we will be able to grieve together.

We can't deliver our children from death itself, or the pain of
death, but only from the fear of death. Hebrews 2:14-15 reminds
us that Christ's sacrifice is what ultimately makes it possible to
face our fear: "Since the children have flesh and blood, he too shared
in their humanity so that by his death he might destroy him who
holds the power of death—that is, the devil—and free those who
all their lives were held in slavery by their fear of death."

The sting of death is gone, and the victory of the grave is hollow,
for neither can separate us from the love of God.

—18—

Stewardship, Consumerism & Greed

Children want to own or control everything that appeals to them, but that isn't possible or even desirable. Children can learn that needs are to be distinguished from wants and that many things can be shared or done without.

One of the first words children learn is "Mine!" but they don't understand the significance of that claim. From their viewpoint "mine" means that they have the exclusive right to control the use and disposition of their toy, blanket or stuffed animal. It's their *possession*. Possessions, unfortunately, do just that: They slowly come to possess our time, our energy, our money, our interest and even our devotion.

Gigapets or Gods?

"But, Mom, all my friends have at least one," Jennifer said, "and they talk about them all the time, and then I have nothing to talk about with them. I just don't see why I can't have just one!"

This question was often repeated in our home shortly after the gigapet craze hit the streets. It was true: all of our daughter's friends did have at least one gigapet. We had told Jennifer that we felt that they were a waste of money, energy and time, especially since she already had several live pets that needed to be fed, played with, loved, cleaned up and taken to the vet. And in taking care of them she received love—from warm, cuddly friends who sought her out on their own initiative.

That wasn't enough for her. We persisted in explaining that gigapets were just a fancy electronic way to separate unsuspecting (or simply gullible) children from their money and make them think that they got the better end of the deal. (Ha!) Madison Avenue will do anything to get money, and if they can encourage a "spend money so I can be cool" attitude in young people, then they (Madison Avenue) will have a whole generation of life-long consumers addicted to being cool, and that will translate into big bucks for them (again, Madison Avenue).

We said that we saw no worthwhile purpose in her having a gigapet (and that being different was a strength). She persisted in asking us if we were saying that she would absolutely never ever be able to have one. We said, "No, we're not saying that, but what we are saying is that we will have to see a purpose for the purchase, and at this moment we don't see one."

One day our daughter, demonstrating her character quality of determination, asked us to clarify just why we didn't want her to have a gigapet, besides the high moral reasons we had already given. "Okay," Mom said, "it goes like this. Kids carry these things everywhere, and whenever they beep, the kid has to suddenly drop what they are doing to 'care' for this piece of plastic with electronic innards so they won't lose points and have the thing die on them. That means that the toy is something like a god—whatever it needs or even wants it gets. It has a slave always ready to do its slightest bidding, and if the slave doesn't, the slave is punished by the score going down."

Jennifer pointed out that she enjoyed caring for little critters and was willing to learn to care for something "on demand." Since this discussion was on going, we talked and decided that perhaps we should recognize the force of her logic and allow her to have one (emphasis on the singular) and establish some strong ground rules to go with it.

So we did.

Rule zero: It had to be a "real" critter—no aliens or unnatural beings.

Rule 1: She had to pay for the thing herself.

Rule 2: The gigapet had to be turned off (silenced) at bedtime or any time Mom or Dad decided it should be simply seen and not heard. (We'd heard about all her friends being woken up in the night to feed their pets!)

Rule 3: No gigapet at the meal table, at school, at church or at music lessons.

Rule 4: No gigapet if Mom and Dad decide they're sick of it.

Rule 5: If any of the above rules were broken, the gigapet would be confiscated for at least two weeks.

Our daughter agreed to all of the rules without question. So she bought herself a gigapet. She hooked it on her belt and took very good care of it when she wasn't in school, eating or practicing her music. We were pleased with the way she managed it. Of course, when she turned it off, she couldn't hear it beeping, so it only "lived" for two or three days at a time. But she persisted and over a long weekend was able to keep it alive for four days.

We rarely saw the thing. Andrew saw that we had allowed her to have one, so he asked for one for his birthday, promising to abide by the same rules. We said, "Not with our money!" so one of his little friends got it for him. Andrew couldn't keep his alive for more than two days. It became common for him to get up in the morning, look at his gigapet and see a little angel flapping its wings. (For the uninitiated, that means it died.)

Within six weeks the gigapets were put away in drawers, all but forgotten, and our children had learned a small lesson that we hope will ring in their memory when they are faced with a similar sort of choice over a much larger issue. Perhaps the next time it will be the latest sport shoes on sale for $139.99 that will be unsuitable and spend their life in the back of the closet. But if they can learn these sorts of lessons with $12 purchases or even with a $140 purchase, it will help save them a lot of money and grief in the future. It will help them save face, too, and some self-respect.

These events gave us a chance to talk about ownership and about good and bad reasons to buy things.

We discussed some unacceptable reasons to "have":

☐ Everybody else has one, and we don't want to be the last.

☐ Nobody else has one, and we can be the first.

On the other hand, there are acceptable reasons to "have":

☐ To make a useful item accessible to others. We bought a portable sump pump to clear out our basement after a drain clogged. We could have rented one, but we felt that we knew several people who might need to borrow one—and when you need a sump pump, you need one *now,* regardless of whether the stores are open. Our expectations were justified; that one pump has rescued several different basements from the effects of flooding—and many of the needs arose in the middle of the night.

☐ To preserve something that might otherwise be lost. Dan has assembled a decent collection of George MacDonald books—many of them over a hundred years old and long out of print. The books are hard to find, and Dan has been able to use them in his writing efforts; he edited a number of the books for "today's readers," making them available to people who couldn't find or afford the originals.

☐ To have ready access to something not otherwise available when needed. Dan tries not to buy books that can be borrowed or consulted elsewhere, but much of his writing and research is accomplished in the wee hours of darkness—times when libraries aren't open.

☐ To extend or complete a collection of something that brings us special pleasure. Jennifer is collecting certain Beanie Babies, while

Andrew has begun assembling the original series of Hardy Boys books. There are limitations, though: such interests are hobbies and can't be allowed to override life's priorities.

☐ As an investment, with a caveat. Elizabeth picks up pink Depression glass when she finds it, with an eye for trading the available pieces for the items she really wants. She knows that the market may dry up suddenly and leave her with her current stock of pink Depression glass, but that's an acceptable risk. She does not buy what she does not like and would display any item happily—it's not just a cold-hearted, speculative investment.

Stewardship—Ownership with Open Hands

When Jennifer was a baby, she seemed to latch on to a certain blanket, so we made it her "blankie." When Andrew came along, he had one too, and they were affectionately known as their "blankies." We told the children that although they would be expected to share their toys and possessions at various times with other people, they would never have to share their blankies. This gave them a sense of security and a sense of control over at least one thing in their young lives. But later on they did share them on special occasions, completely of their own volition.

(Jennifer at three and a half) *Grieving for my father hits hard some days. Today after I put Andrew down for his nap and before I could get you settled, I crashed on my bed and the tears came. I'm so tired and I miss Dad so much. I cannot imagine this world without him in it, yet he's been gone now for a month, so I guess the world is getting along without him. I'm not managing very well, though. You came in to see me, and when you saw the tears on my face, you stopped, looked more carefully and, without saying a word, disappeared only to return a moment later with your blankie. You held it out to me and said, 'Here, Mommy.' I was so touched by your care. You recognized that I needed comfort, so you offered to me what brings yourself comfort, your precious blankie. Thank you, sweetie. I'll never forget your simple gesture of care. It's a real example for me. And by the way, it did help me feel better!*

Andrew desperately wanted the Blue Angel G.I. Joe figure but didn't have enough money saved up to buy it. Dan wasn't sure it would still be available when the money was, so he secretly went back to the store and bought the toy. Elizabeth put it away, thinking that if he didn't pay for it himself we could give it to him for Christmas.

But Andrew's intent and determination did not wane, and he diligently saved his allowance and extra money for that stated purpose. When he was finally able to count out $26.24 from his piggy bank, he started asking if we could go to the store and get the Blue Angel.

Dan decided to try a little game with him.

"Do you trust me enough to give me your money?" he asked Andrew.

He nodded and brought the money to Dan.

"You'll never see this money again," Dan warned.

"Okay," our son said, mightily puzzled, and perhaps a bit apprehensive but still willing to play it through.

Dan put the money in his wallet and then pointed to Elizabeth, who had crept into the room with the package hidden behind her back.

"No, we won't go to the store—we don't have to. We already bought it, and you can buy it from us. We wanted you to have one when you had the money set aside."

Andrew was delighted and thanked Dan at least ten times that day alone for his actions.

But not all our stories involve happy circumstances, even if there is an eternal purpose hidden behind it.

Elizabeth had given Andrew a "bomber jacket" when he was eight, a recognition of his interest in World War 2 aviation history, an item that he wore proudly and frequently whenever the weather was cool enough. The jacket was recently stolen from church. It was upsetting for all of us, but we were able to pray that God would accomplish something good through this—whether to teach us to be more careful, to challenge us on where we placed our affections, to convict the individual who took it or to press for changes in the location and safety of the church coat racks ... anything that might show God's sovereignty.

Our first responsibility was to help Andrew react properly to the loss. He listened to our discussions and prayers, and though he cried over its disappearance, he did thank Elizabeth for getting it for him. And in touching recognition of the fact that Dan was without a job, he said, "I know we could probably find another one somewhere, but I don't think I want one until Daddy gets another job." (It cuts us adults to the quick sometimes to be exposed to a child's generous heart.)

We all talked about the situation and realized that we had to forgive the thief—whoever the person was and for whatever reasons he or she had taken it. They were hard words to say out loud, but saying them made the emotional commitment a little easier.

The next Sunday we arrived at church and discovered that the jacket had been returned, anonymously and with no explanation. We placed it in Andrew's grateful arms and thanked God for the returned gift and the lessons learned.

(That story had a happy ending, but not all of them do. We're still missing a pair of kid's bicycles, a car radio and a Canadian flag.)

Wise consumers are savvy shoppers, but they are not consumed by their possessions. We want our children to use things in the service of people and not use people in the service of things.

—19—

The Love
of Laughter (and
the Laughter
of Love)

The mixture of love and laughter frees us from crippling our dignity and enables us to keep our problems in perspective.

Our adherence to principles gives us immense freedom within the established boundaries, and our house frequently erupts with merriment. There is constant wordplay and patter of puns, jokes, riddles and wry comments; there are playful pillow fights and mock wrestling matches. Laughter is a healing sound, and we love to hear Dan's snorts of amusement, Elizabeth's peals of laughter, Jennifer's giggles and Andrew's shrieks of pleasure.

Our aim—and our privilege—is to indulge in the worthwhile and joyful things God sends our way every day, to laugh at ourselves and with each other, to observe the ironic and comment on the absurd without stooping to sarcasm. Laughter is a loving lubricant that makes life together possible and much more pleasant.

Jennifer tends to be overdramatic, and sometimes the best way to defuse that is to beat her to the punch. She rushed into the room the other day and proclaimed with breathless intensity that she had just found a flea on one of the cats. Dan wasn't in the mood to humor her histrionics, so he got there first. "Oh no!" he exclaimed. "What ever shall we do? Get the shotgun and load it with flea powder! Break out the sheep dip! Call 911!" Jennifer started laughing and realized that maybe one little flea wasn't worth the reaction she was giving it.

We will *all* have our dignities punctured somewhere along the time; it's a question of *when*, not *if.* Not even Dad and Mom get the best of it every time.

When Andrew was four, Elizabeth was sick one day; she allowed him to pull out his play "doctor kit" and examine her to see what was wrong. He did all the standard things: taking her temperature, feeling her forehead and tapping her knee to check her reflexes. Then he peered into her ear and said, "Oooo!"

"What's wrong?"

"Buggies! *Lots* of buggies!" He was repeating something he had heard us say when examining the stray cats that came around. He had in mind a prescription for ear mite medicine, but the dose of laughter he unwittingly dispensed was far more effective as well as a great illustration of Proverbs 17:22: "A cheerful heart is good medicine."

Hey!
We have come to enjoy what we call the "Hey!" moments—the times when a wisecrack or obtuse comment *almost* gets by the audience, and gets a reaction when it's caught.

Both children were sprawled on the floor, using a piece of string to amuse one of our new kittens. They would tug on one end, the other end would twitch as though it were alive, and the kitten would pounce eagerly but inexpertly on it. As Dan walked by, Jennifer said, "Look, Dad, she likes to play with the little jerks!"

Dan replied, "So I see—and with the string, too." He was three steps past them before his words sunk in. Jennifer sat up and said "Hey! What did you just call us?" unable to decide whether to be amused or insulted.

Dan came back and knelt down. "I didn't call you anything; I just agreed with your analysis of the situation. Seriously, I have never called you guys jerks or any other nasty names, and that's what makes it so funny now. I just couldn't pass that one up."

They understood, laughed at the humor and tucked the memory away. Now it's one of the first stories they tell their friends or our visitors when the subject of kittens comes up. They're not afraid to laugh at themselves.

If we are secure in our identities as God's children and beloved family members, we don't have to take ourselves seriously. We can admit that we sometimes *act* like fools and idiots and morons, knowing all the time that we are *not* fools and idiots and morons.

Jennifer came to us once with a bump on her forehead and a sheepish grin on her face.

"What happened to you?" we asked.

"I tried to walk through the front door before I opened it," she replied. "I was thinking about something else and got mixed up which to do first."

Humor—serious humor—can also defuse tense situations.

The kids sat at the dinner table and looked gloomily at their plates. "Casserole again? Can't I have something else?" one of them said.

"Feel free to wrestle the cats for some cat food," said Elizabeth, smiling, but with an edge to her voice. "You don't have to eat the casserole, but I'm not cooking anything else."

It gradually dawned on the kids that although Elizabeth was joking, she was not kidding. Yes there was plenty of food in the house, but the only meals prepared were the casserole and the cat food. They could have their choice, or do without supper at all. It wasn't funny to them at that point, but as they've grown older they've discovered the humor in it. Now when one of them complains about the choice on the dinner table, all we have to do is say, "Help yourself to the cat food, then." They get the point, they smile wryly, and they stop complaining—out loud, anyway.

Sometimes the stories the kids tell at the dinner table tend to drift toward the superlative and the unbelievable, prompting one parent or the other to lean forward and exclaim, "I've told you a million times not to exaggerate!" They get that point, too, and choose their words a bit more carefully.

But laughter can be cruel if we pass from laughing with someone to laughing at them. The only way to stay on the right side of this line of distinction is to know one another. There are some things Jennifer can laugh about and some she can't. The same applies to Andrew—and for us adults as well. As we grow, we gain perspective and tolerance for what are foibles but not sins.

The rules are always changing, and life isn't always easy, but a little bit of laughter based on love and personal knowledge can go a long way to ease friction. C. S. Lewis called the Christian life a dance, and it is in this dance that we remember his words: "Joy is the serious business of heaven."

—20—

A Curious
Blessing

*The ultimate responsibility for life's attitudes,
choices and actions falls upon
the grown child, and there is a time
when we the parents must let go of them.
However, there are Scriptures that give us hope
that our efforts will not be in vain.*

We were in a discussion at church about "endangered kids"
when we began to wonder what the opposite was. Safe
kids? Good kids? Not necessarily.

We finally settled on "dangerous kids," because it's not the world
that threatens to change these kids, but these kids who will one
day threaten to change the world.

Endangered Kids

We decided that "endangered kids" generally have the following
characteristics:

1. They are at risk from the world. Peer pressure and media
influence will greatly determine the shape of their lives. They will
tend to be followers rather than leaders.

2. They are insecure and vulnerable. Their identity is firmly
rooted in . . . what? Their dependence on anything temporary or

variable (popularity, skills, success) will disappoint them in the end.

3. They are lost in their world and largely indistinguishable from the others in it. They feel that they are all alone, misunderstood and unwanted; they find it easier to fit in than to find their own niche.

4. They are uninformed, gullible and naive. They may have the facts, but they have not acquired the truth and understanding that makes knowledge out of facts and wisdom out of knowledge. If they have opinions, they are either inherited from family members or acquired from peers and remain unexamined.

5. If they are innocent, it is largely due to ignorance, apathy or circumstance. Their lack of involvement in an attractive but dubious activity is limited only by their knowledge or their ability to participate.

Dangerous Kids

Then we decided that "dangerous kids," in contrast, should have the following general characteristics:

1. They are likely to change the world. They tend to ignore or discount peer pressure and the natterings of the media. They tend to be leaders, which could be either good or bad depending on what they lead others into!

2. They are secure and confident. Their identity is rooted in their status as children of God and the beloved offspring of their parents. Their confidence in their special place in God's plan is not shattered when their world changes for the worse.

3. They are insulated (but not isolated). They will take their share of lumps from being in the world, even though they're not of it. But their ability to survive will be greatly enhanced by the realization that they are not alone in the world, they are not unwanted, and they are not the first people in history to face the problems of growing up.

4. They are informed and alert. They have gathered the relevant facts and followed the path from facts to knowledge to truth to wisdom. They have examined their acquired or inherited opinions to determine if they are worth upholding.

5. *They display innocence born of knowledge and choice.* They understand quite clearly that just because they *can* do something doesn't mean that they *should.*

A "dangerous child" is a risk, of course, because even the best can go bad; the highest angels made the worst demons. But it is a risk worth taking, for even God found it worthwhile to create and raise people who could turn their backs on him.

"Train a Child in the Way He Should Go . . . He Will Not Turn from It"

What kind of word from God is this injunction from Proverbs 22:6? Is this an iron-clad promise? We've heard it claimed as such, with anger by parents when their children go astray.

It isn't fully a commandment, and it isn't quite a promise. It's *wisdom*—an observation that "this is how things generally go." It means that the lifestyle, beliefs, morals and convictions of the average adult will reflect what he or she was taught as a "little one."

Our kids aren't perfect, but they're great. They're occasionally stubborn but not rebellious, intermittently irritating but not permanently obnoxious; they give us headaches but not heartaches. We think they understand God's love for them and realize he has a plan for their lives, but we don't know what actions they will eventually take on the strength of that knowledge.

This is our hope, that our children will follow in the path of the wisdom we've showered upon them. Neither Andrew or Jennifer are ready to leave the nest yet, but each day they're making more of their own decisions, shouldering more of the consequences and readying themselves for independence. As grown children they will be ultimately responsible for their beliefs, choices and actions before God.

From Elizabeth's diaries:

I pray for protection for my babies. No, they are far past being babies, but when I creep into their rooms at night and watch them sleeping, I still see the sweet innocence of a two-year old, and they are once again my babies. I ask God to protect their bodies—from disease, accidents, their own carelessness and people who would harm them. I ask God to protect their minds, that they will grow in their knowledge and understanding of him and his wonderful world and its laws, but not be led astray by academic discussion over too many why's—that they would hold fast to their faith. I pray that they will be protected from Satan's attacks, that their guardian angels will be strengthened to fight for them in the invisible arena of spirits, and that their father and I would become wiser and wiser as we lead them to the path they will walk on their own.

I pray for their future husband and wife, that whoever they are, they too will be protected and guarded in all their ways and that they and their families will be kept from things that could contribute to difficulties in future relationships. I pray that if they are not yet Christians, they will very soon come to know Jesus Christ so they can begin now the patterns and lifestyle that will make them better mates and parents, and productive, happy Christians.

And I thank God for the health and strength of my children, their fresh ideas, their enthusiasm and curiosity—all his provision for being a child.

A Challenge, Not a Warranty

When Peter inquired about his future, Jesus said,

> "I tell you the truth, when you were younger you dressed yourself and went where you wanted; but when you are old you will stretch out your hands, and someone else will dress you and lead you where you do not want to go." Jesus said this to indicate the kind of death by which Peter would glorify God. Then he said to him, "Follow me!"
>
> Peter turned and saw that the disciple whom Jesus loved was following them. (This was the one who had leaned back against Jesus at the supper and had said, "Lord, who is going to betray you?") When Peter saw him, he asked, "Lord, what about him?"

> Jesus answered, "If I want him to remain alive until I return, what is that to you? You must follow me." Because of this, the rumor spread among the brothers that this disciple would not die. But Jesus did not say that he would not die; he only said, "If I want him to remain alive until I return, what is that to you?" (John 21:18-23)

In other words, "His fate is none of your business, and you will receive no promises concerning him. Your business is your reaction to me and your relationships with me."

We're back to where we started—realizing that our prime responsibility is living our lives for God and not trying to live our children's lives for them.

It isn't too difficult to guide a child who loves and respects you, who loves to be with you and hangs on almost every word you say. However, that stage doesn't last long. They quickly learn that they don't have to listen and obey. The negative consequences of their lack of obedience will help convince them to be more careful in the future. But as they grow they become their own little persons, and I wonder sometimes if all that we have taught our children will blow up in our faces when they get to be fifteen. What then, if we've done everything we know to guide them properly? It could happen, and it would be painful beyond our ability to imagine now.

But we're not without hope, or the glimpses of possible rewards, for God has his own plans:

> As the rain and the snow come down from heaven, and do not return to it without watering the earth and making it bud and flourish, so that it yields seed for the sower and bread for the eater, so is my word that goes out from my mouth: It will not return to me empty, but will accomplish what I desire and achieve the purpose for which I sent it. (Isaiah 55:10-11)

Dan was proud when Andrew, at nine, offered to say grace for himself and his non-Christian friend at the local pizza restaurant. (They had insisted on a separate table for themselves, which was fine with Dan—he was trying to finish the final chapters of this book! And the material was right in front of him all the time!)

There were lots of giggles and whispering involved, but there was a brief prayer in the middle somewhere. Who was it done for? Not for Dan, but hopefully for God because Andrew knew it pleased him and we "always did it that way."

"And a little child shall lead them."

An A-B-Z of Reminders

Simple lists may help remind us of the things we already know but forget to put into daily practice.

Bravely into the Future ...
Analyze your kids' environment—know their interests.
Be consistent.
Communicate cautions.
Demonstrate your beliefs and convictions.
Educate them as you grow together.
Force yourself to be accessible—*listen* when they talk.
Give kids the freedoms they earn.
Hug them a lot.
Invest yourself in your kids.
Join in their activities.
Keep the eternal perspective in mind.
Laugh frequently and together.
Mind your marriage.
Never give up.
Opportunities are for grabbing.
Pray for and with them regularly.
Questions deserve answers.
Read to them and share your special memories.
Smile into their eyes every day.
Teach them God's Word.
Understand the pressure from their peers.
Voice your love and pride in them.
Wonder with them; see the universe through their eyes.
Xpress confidence in them.
You are the adult—set the example!
Zip your lip about the tiny things—overlook the insignificant.

Further Reading

Other people have walked the perilous road of parenthood and not only survived but wrote down their wisdom for our benefit.

Of course no one book can say it all, and there is no shortage of printed opinions, theories and experiences. These other resources might be helpful in fleshing out the approach you wish to take with your children. (Note that not all of these books reflect a Christian viewpoint or even a viewpoint endorsed by us; they do, however, provide useful information and alternative ideas worth discussing and understanding.)

Anderson, Ray S. *Everything That Makes Me Happy I Learned when I Grew Up.* Downers Grove, Ill.: InterVarsity Press, 1995.

Arterburn, Stephen, and Jim Burns. *Drug-Proof Your Kids.* Dallas: Focus on the Family/Word, 1989.

Broadman, Muriel. *Understanding Your Child's Entertainment.* New York: Harper & Row, 1977.

Campbell, Ross. *How to Really Love Your Child.* Wheaton, Ill.: Victor, 1977.

———. *How to Really Love Your Teenager.* Wheaton, Ill.: Victor, 1981.

———. *How to Really Love Your Children.* Wheaton, Ill.: Victor, 1981. (A combination of the two books listed above.)

Cantor, Joanne. *Mommy, I'm Scared: How TV and Movies Frighten Children and What We Can Do to Protect Them.* Orlando, Fla.: Harvest/Harcourt Brace, 1998.

Fuller, Cheri. *Helping Your Child Succeed in Public School.* Colorado Springs, Colo.: Focus on the Family, 1993.

Gore, Tipper. *Raising PG Kids in an X-Rated World.* Nashville: Abingdon, 1987.

Hughes, Donna Rice. *Kids Online: Protecting Your Children in Cyberspace.* Grand Rapids, Mich.: Baker/Revell, 1998.

Johnson, Victoria and Mike Murphy. *Parenting Streetwise Kids.* Elgin, Ill.: David C. Cook, 1995.

Kindig, Eileen Silva. *Remember the Time . . . ? The Power and Promise of Family Storytelling.* Downers Grove, Ill.: InterVarsity Press, 1997.

Korem, Dan. *Streetwise Parents, Foolproof Kids.* Colorado Springs, Colo.: NavPress, 1992.

Lea, Larry. *Wisdom: Don't Live Life Without It.* Nashville: Oliver-Nelson, 1990.

Leman, Kevin. *Parenthood Without Hassles (Well, Almost).* Eugene, Ore.: Harvest House, 1979.

Maddoux, Marilyn. *What Worries Parents Most.* Eugene, Ore.: Harvest House, 1992.

McDill, Rutherford, and Ronald Stephens. *Raising Safety-Smart Kids.* Nashville: Thomas Nelson, 1993.

McDowell, Josh, and Bob Hostetler. *Right from Wrong: What You Need to Know to Help Youth Make Right Choices.* Dallas: Word, 1994.

Michaelson, Johanna. *Like Lambs to the Slaughter.* Eugene, Ore.: Harvest House, 1989.

Miranker, Cathy, and Alison Elliot. *Great Software for Kids and Parents.* Foster City, Calif.: IDG Books, 1996.

Schimmels, Cliff. *Parent's Most-Asked Questions About Kids and Schools.* Wheaton, Ill.: Victor, 1989.

White, Joe. *Orphans at Home.* Phoenix, Ariz.: Questar, 1988.

Wilson, Sandra D. *Shame-Free Parenting.* Downers Grove, Ill.: InterVarsity Press, 1992.

Youth for Christ. *How to Raise Christian Kids in a Non-Christian World.* Wheaton, Ill.: Victor, 1988.